When Louis XIV died in 1715, he had reigned for seventy-two years. He had dominated European history for most of that time. The "Sun King" is remembered as the builder of the magnificent palace at Versailles, and as the man who plunged Europe into repeated wars in his quest for personal glory. He was indeed vain and arrogant, and supremely confident that kings were not like other men. But he did not see himself as a wicked tyrant: "When God raised Kings to their thrones, he intended that they should do their duty."

How far could Louis live up to the almost god-like image that he presented to his subjects? How did he cope with a style of life that made his getting up and going to bed daily public ceremonies? Christopher Martin tells of the strange education that fitted the boy king for his rôle – of how, from the age of five, he was made to copy out maxims such as "Homage is due to kings; they do as they please."

This biography explains how Louis, despite all the pleasures and luxuries that were available for him, worked six hours every day for what he saw as the good of his country – but completely failed to make those changes which French society so desperately needed. A courtier wrote of "this kingdom whose one great pleasure is to behold its master," and Louis never questioned that view. Christopher Martin gives a fascinating impression of the life of a king who was all-powerful, but who was cut off by his rank from contact with the real world.

Louis XIV

Christopher Martin

"He had an elevation in his soul that bore him
towards great things." Voltaire, *The Great Age
of Louis XIV*
"The life of the King was a perpetual delusion."
Saint-Simon, *Memoirs*

WAYLAND PUBLISHERS

Wayland Kings and Queens

Alfred the Great	Jennifer Westwood
Henry VIII	David Fletcher
Mary Queen of Scots	Alan Bold
Elizabeth I	Alan Kendall
James I	David Walter
Charles I	Hugh Purcell
Charles II	Michael Gibson
Queen Victoria	Richard Garrett
Louis XIV	Christopher Martin
Napoleon I	Stephen Pratt
Charlemagne	Keith Ellis
Charles V	William Rayner
Wilhelm II	Richard Garrett
Peter the Great	Michael Gibson
Catherine the Great	Miriam Kochan

Frontispiece Louis XIV as a young
man. The painter, Pierre Mignard,
has shown him in one of his favourite
poses, as a triumphant Roman
general.

SBN 85340 390 2

© Copyright 1975 by Wayland (Publishers) Ltd,
49 Lansdowne Place, Hove, East Sussex.
Filmset by Keyspools Limited, Golborne, Lancs.
Printed in Great Britain by
The Pitman Press Limited, Bath.

Contents

1 Louis the God-given

ON 5TH SEPTEMBER, 1638, at the Château of Saint-Germain, outside Paris, a baby son was born to Anne of Austria, wife of the King of France, Louis XIII. It seemed a miracle after twenty-two years of a cold and childless marriage. The baby, after being washed in wine and oil of red roses, was baptized with the auspicious name of Louis. The outlook for the future of France seemed bright once more. Louis XIII and his minister Cardinal Richelieu had given the state a new strength and self-respect, but People could still remember the Religious Wars of the previous century, and feared a return to the thirty years of anarchy. Now, there was a long hoped-for Dauphin to inherit the throne and give the country security. In fact the child was to grow into a king who would dominate Europe for the rest of the century and beyond.

Fifty special couriers carried the news of the birth across France, and wild excitement spread over the country. Paris celebrated with six days of delirious joy. Religious processions sang *Te Deum* in the streets; bells rang; the Militia fired salvoes from their muskets; cannon thundered from the Bastille. Crowds danced in the street, singing, "Now we have a Dauphin." At night, the sky was lit by bonfires and hundreds of fire-work displays. A Paris news-sheet, *La Gazette*, described the street feasts: "people stove in casks of wine . . . and invited all passers-by to have a drink, asking no payment but a cry of 'Long live the King'." Fountains poured out wine instead of water. A rich Parisian toured the city with carts full of musicians playing, while servants gave out free meat and pastries. The

"France is filled with a sure hope of the most signal favour she has received in this august and wonderful reign, namely the birth of a Dauphin, for which this year has been set apart by God." *The newspaper "Mercure François" announcing Anne of Austria's pregnancy.*

Opposite Louis XIV as a child of eleven, wearing his state robes.

Below Louis XIII, Louis XIV's father, King of France 1610–43.

fortibus Armis
e Iura De

great houses of Paris were a blaze of light as nobles and foreign ambassadors competed to put on the most lavish entertainments. "All this jollity had to be seen to be believed," concluded *La Gazette*. The royal fortune-teller announced that the sun had actually moved nearer the earth on Louis' birthday "to share the happy event." A specially-coined medal showed the rising sun of France, a symbol connected with Louis throughout his life.

Foreign kings and princes dutifully sent their congratulations, secretly hoping that when Louis XIII died, as they expected he soon would. France would be ruled by a weak Regent until the child King grew up. However, the vigour of the baby boy impressed observers: one ambassador noted that the infant had been born with two teeth, which seemed a portent of "his power to bite his neighbours." Another noticed his appetite and wrote, "Let France's neighbours beware of such precocious greed." Of the many gifts sent from abroad, that from Pope Urban VIII was the most splendid: baby clothes of silk, finest linen, Flemish lace and cloth of silver embroidered with gold thread. Humbler friends of France also sent gifts. The Indians of New France in Canada sent a beaded outfit for an Indian papoose to "our Good King."

Queen Anne, delighted at being a mother at last, poured out on her baby the love she could not give to her weak, cold-blooded husband. "The Queen hardly ever leaves the little Dauphin," reported a lady of the court. "She delights in playing with him and in taking him for drives when it is fine. He is her principal pleasure . . ." This devotion soon spread to the rest of the court. So began the cult of the future "Sun King".

2 The Condition of France

THE FRANCE INTO WHICH LOUIS WAS BORN was in a good position to become the strongest power in Europe. Its population was rising, and by 1700 was 18 million, compared to the 14 million of Russia, the $6\frac{1}{2}$ million of Austria (nearly 20 million in the entire Austrian Empire), the 6 million of Spain and the $5\frac{1}{2}$ million of England. It was a geographical unity, with rich, varied and fruitful land and a pleasant climate. "Heaven itself has given the nation almost miraculous gifts," wrote an Italian envoy. "It is full of fertile land, excellently situated upon two oceans, watered by many navigable rivers which flow in all directions . . . it is rich in wealth and soldiers."

Yet France was backward, compared with more efficient and prosperous rivals like Holland or England. Its agriculture was still medieval. Wooden ploughs and spades were still common. Crop yields were low and uncertain – rich landlords didn't need to take any interest in the science of farming, and poor peasants could not afford to – and even the rotation of crops was barely known. France's resources of coal and metal lay unexploited, and tools and weapons were bought abroad. Poor roads made transport painfully slow, and rivers were choked and unusable; local customs duties, sometimes levied at the borders of every parish, made trade difficult and unprofitable.

France was further held back by its rigid class divisions. The peasantry still formed the bulk of the population. Dressed in coarse cloth, with wooden clogs, living in thatched hovels, they lived simply at the best of times, on a meatless diet of bread and dripping, and porridge.

Below A typical French peasant with his few animals and his tools. The caption says he is "born to suffer".

9

Right A contemporary cartoon compares the relationship of the noble and the peasant with that of the spider and the fly.

> "Certain wild creatures, male and female, are to be seen about the countryside, grimy, livid, burnt black by the sun, as though tethered to the soil which they dig and till with unconquerable tenacity . . . When they stand upright, they show a human face; they are, in fact, men. At night they creep back into dens, where they live on black bread, water and roots; they spare other men the trouble of sowing, ploughing and reaping in order to live, and they deserve not to go short of that bread which they have sown . . ."
> *La Bruyère on the peasants, in "Characters".*

> "Great nobles pride themselves on cutting an avenue through a forest, on building long retaining walls for an estate, on gilding ceilings, on conveying a foot of water to their pools, on stocking an orangery; but as for bringing contentment to a human heart, filling another's soul with joy, forestalling extreme need or remedying it, their interest does not extend that far . . ." *La Bruyère on the nobility, in "Characters".*

As much as half the value of their crops might go to the landlord in rent; or if, as was common in Southern France, they owned their own smallholding, it was often too tiny to keep them above the level of starvation. The periodic scourges were famine, plague and war. Not surprisingly the peasant's expectation of life at birth was only twenty-five years.

At the other end of the social scale were the nobility, whose wealth was based on land, which they had inherited from their medieval ancestors. They lived on the rents paid by the peasants, and these rents were often fixed for all time. This wealth had therefore sunk considerably during the sixteenth century, owing to the huge price inflation and fall in the value of money caused by Spanish gold imports from America. This

Above A group of prosperous Paris merchants.

loss of status explains the restlessness of the nobility in the seventeenth century. Their fixed incomes were cut, yet they were expected to keep up a life of elaborate display.

The new power in the land was the middle class, making its money from trade. A member of this *bourgeoisie*, having made his fortune in business, could buy himself an official post, even a noble title for his family. Although still few in numbers and confined to the large towns, the middle class began to play a large part in the running of the state. Most of the great ministers of Louis XIV's reign were bourgeois in origin.

The King was only gradually being accepted as the main source of authority in France. A French King of early medieval times had been merely an elected leader

Above Merchants doing business on the dockside, while behind them labourers unload bales of cloth.

Below Two peasants eat a frugal meal of bread and wine.

among fellow princes of equal status, who ruled other provinces in the land (the "royal domain" around Paris being one of the smallest). Only after long struggles did the French Kings emerge by 1500 as "absolute" rulers of the whole of France, passing on their titles to their sons. The power of the monarchy was again lost during the Wars of Religion (1563–1593) between Catholics and Protestants (called "Huguenots" in France). These wars had also devastated much of the country, leaving the peasants on the edge of starvation and setting back the growth of commerce. Henry IV (1589–1610), a Huguenot convert to Catholicism, first of the Bourbon kings and Louis XIV's grandfather, had ended the civil war by his Edict of Nantes (1598) which gave Huguenots freedom of worship, the right to hold official posts, and the right to hold and fortify certain towns. Henry then set about restoring the royal power and strengthening the French economy. He had only begun his work when an assassin stabbed him to death in 1610.

During the reign of his son, Louis XIII (1601–1643), who preferred hunting to government, France was really ruled, after 1624, by his First Minister, Cardinal Richelieu (1585–1642). Richelieu promised Louis that he would make all the King's subjects respect his authority. The Huguenots, who had become "a state within a state" since the Edict of Nantes, were crushed by force, following a rebellion in 1627. They retained only their freedom of worship. Richelieu continually battled with rebellious nobles led by the King's brother, Gaston d'Orleans, and the Queen-Mother, Marie de Medicis. He outplayed them, forcing them into exile or disgrace. He also attacked the provinces and towns that regarded themselves as nearly independent by appointing *Intendants*, government officials who ruled in place of the local noblemen.

Abroad, Richelieu's policy was "to lift the King's name in foreign countries to the place it ought to hold." The brutal Thirty Years' War had been raging in Germany since 1618. The Hapsburg Archduke of Austria, who was also Holy Roman Emperor and so the overlord of Germany, was trying to win back to the Catholic faith those German States which had become Protestant since the Reformation. The Hapsburgs of Vienna were allied to the Hapsburgs of Spain, who ruled Flanders, Franche-Comte, parts of Italy and most of South America. France, although a Catholic country, disliked this Hapsburg encirclement and feared what might happen if Austria won the war. Richelieu therefore supported the German Protestant states, and, in 1635, France declared war on Spain, hoping to secure those Spanish provinces on her borders that threatened her security. Richelieu died with his work unfinished, but the Treaties of Westphalia of 1648 saw France extend her frontiers to the north and east.

The early years of the seventeenth century had, then, seen the other Great Powers of Europe in decline. In France, the idea that the King should have absolute authority, under God, over all his subjects, had been widely accepted. Louis was brought up with that idea, and was to exercise that authority in a way that had never before been possible.

Left Cardinal Richelieu, chief minister of Louis XIII from 1624 to 1642.

13

3 The Boy King

IN MAY, 1643, LOUIS XIII FELL SERIOUSLY ILL. The official baptism of the Dauphin was quickly arranged. On his return from the ceremony, the dying king asked his son what his new name was. "Louis XIV," was the reply. "Not yet, not yet," answered his father sadly. When he died, his son became king, while still only four years old.

His mother, after proudly kissing the boy "who was both her child and her King," took Louis on a solemn entry into Paris. Enthusiastic crowds greeted the new monarch. "What struck the spectators most of all was the expression of precocious gravity on the face of the young king," noted one eye witness, while *La Gazette* reported that he was "beautiful as an angel, displaying in all his actions a modesty and decorum extraordinary in one of his age." At the "Parlement" of Paris (not elected, like the English Parliament, but a council of important lawyers who advised the king), Louis was officially presented. His mother was made Regent, with "free, absolute and entire administration of the affairs of his kingdom during his minority." Anne was not clever enough to rule herself, and soon appointed another Cardinal, Jules Mazarin (1602–1661), from a humble Italian background, but trained by Richelieu himself, to be Chief Minister.

Mazarin was also Louis' godfather and looked after his education. An elaborate array of tutors gave Louis lessons in Geography, Mathematics, Italian and Spanish, Latin, drawing and writing. He also learned to play the guitar and lute, and dancing, at which he always excelled. Although one report spoke of Louis as "dull

and listless'' in his lessons, and although he described himself later in life as "an ignorant fellow who learned nothing,'' he could do well enough where his interest was engaged. So his boyish love of warfare allowed him to translate Julius Caesar's *Gallic Wars*, a history of the conquest of France by the Romans, to impress his Latin tutor.

The propaganda about his future rôle as king, which surrounded him in his education and his whole life at court, emphasized two points: he would be glorious and all-powerful, but he must never forget the responsibilities which this great power and glory imposed on him. In his writing book he was given sentences to copy such as "Homage is due to Kings; they do as they please.'' His history tutor composed a special life of his grandfather, Henry IV, whose life and work he should

Above Louis XIV attends his first meeting of the Parlement of Paris in 1643. His mother, the regent, sits next to him.

Opposite Cardinal Jules Mazarin, an Italian who became chief minister during the regency of Anne of Austria and was said to be secretly married to her.

15

Above Louis as a child, dressed up as an Arab soldier.

admire. A large map, on the wall of his room at the Palais Royal in Paris, displayed all the places in the world once ruled by his ancestors: France, Naples, Sicily, Portugal, Navarre, Jerusalem, Poland, Germany, even Constantinople. A special pack of cards showed him kings and queens good and bad (his own mother was placed among "the saintly queens"). La Porte, his valet, read him French history, hinting at various kings whom he should imitate or despise. The boy grew angry when it was suggested that he might become another Louis the Sluggard (Louis V).

His religious education was left to his mother, who, reared as a princess at the Spanish court, was a passionate Catholic. Louis took his faith from her: two beliefs, that no-one could disagree with a king appointed by God, and that it was the royal duty to crush heretics (opponents of the true religion), were to have tragic consequences later in his reign. The Queen-Mother's training was fierce: Louis was once locked up for two days for swearing. Even so, he did not grow up to be a fanatical believer; he was able to separate religion from politics, and defy the Pope, supposedly God's representative on earth. At this time Mazarin was carrying on Richelieu's policy of supporting the German Protestants against the Catholic Emperor, and Louis himself was later to do the same.

Louis showed early interest in military affairs. His toys reflected this. He had been presented with model soldiers made of silver, and miniature gold cannon to be drawn by fleas. In the grounds of the Palace, Mazarin had a fort built for Louis and his friends, large enough for them to ride horses through. Here war-games were played, Louis wildly beating a drum or firing small guns, which used real gunpowder. He was taken to see a mock naval battle, which even involved small fire-ships. He loved to review his troops before they departed to the interminable battles of the war against Spain. On a white horse, with pistols at his saddle, the nine-year-old king was to be seen in embroidered coat and plumed hat, with the white sash of a commanding-officer already across his chest. "The young monarch wore a martial air which seemed entirely natural," noted *La Gazette*. His passion for war, which dominated his life, was thus learned early.

Yet there were strange contrasts in the way he lived. His public image was splendid. Madame de Motteville, a court lady, described him, for example, at a dance, dressed in black satin trimmed with gold lace and pink ribbons. "His fine features, his sweet, yet serious, expression, the pink and white of his complexion, and his hair, which was at that time very fair and curly, became him far better than his clothes. He danced perfectly, and . . . he was one of the most distinguished and certainly the most handsome of those present, although he was only eight years old." In private, by contrast, he lived relatively poorly. All his sheets had holes in them, and the upholstery of his coach was worn and tattered. Tradesmen, to whom the Royal Family owed money, threatened to stop providing food. Despite all his tutors, Louis was often quite solitary. Once, left on his own, he nearly drowned in a fountain. Being lonely, he played with a servant's children. His valet's description provides a more human view to set against the public image of the "Sun King": "When he was going to sleep, he would make me put my head on his pillow, and, if he woke in the night, he would creep into my bed . . . I have often carried him back asleep to his own."

LOVIS XIV PAR LA GRACE DE DIEV, ROY DE FRANCE ET DE NAVARRE.
Leüis, qui nous promet le calme apres l'Orage,
Ioint desia des Lauriers à ses Lys Triomphans,
Et par ses actions plus grandes que son aage,
Nous apprend que les Roys ne sont jamais enfans.
B. Moncornet excu.

Above Louis in his early teens. The verse below is already flattering him for his achievements.

Left The notables of France pay homage to the new king. Cardinal Mazarin is second from left.

4 The Frondes

Below A satirical cartoon against Mazarin, showing him leading a band of monopolists dressed as devils who are trying to blow the ship of state of France off course.

PERSONAL EXPERIENCE, more than any classroom lesson, was important in moulding the future King's attitudes. Deep mental scars remained in Louis from the "Frondes," the two civil wars that broke out between 1648 and 1653. A fronde was literally a catapult, used by street urchins to bombard rich people's carriages; when authority appeared, the boys ran away. The name sums up well the method and effect of these last revolts against the King's authority before he took over control of the government in 1661. It was quite usual for the great nobles and other powerful bodies in the state to make trouble during a boy King's minority.

The First Fronde was begun by the Parlements. These were bodies of lawyers, in Paris and the chief provincial cities, who registered the King's edicts as laws, and had some power to object to them. Various grievances drove them to revolt: the Spanish War had increased taxes severely; the *rentes*, the government loan in which middle-class men invested their money, was not paying regular interest because the government, too, was short of cash; the *intendants* were reducing the power of local officials throughout France. Underlying the long list of complaints, presented to the King in 1648, were two basic resentments: against the increased power of the monarchy, and against Mazarin himself, unpopular as the Queen-Mother's "Italian favourite." Although the common people had little to gain from this quarrel, the arrest of a Parlement leader stirred the Paris mob in battle. "The mob has taken up arms," wrote Anne in a letter, "the barricades have been put up in the streets . . . this is only the beginning; the evil may grow to a point where the royal authority will be destroyed." It seemed like a revolution, and reminded the Queen Regent uncomfortably that Charles I of England had been deposed by Parliament and the Army after a bitter civil war, and was soon to lose his head. However, although Cardinal Mazarin was forced to give in to some demands of the Parlements, the Fronde soon collapsed when the nobles came to "help" the rebels. The middle-class "Parlementaires" disliked Mazarin, but not so much as they hated the privileged aristocrats, whose power was built into the system of land-ownership and could not be overthrown.

The second revolt, the Fronde of the Princes, involved the great nobles, like Gaston d'Orleans, the King's uncle, or the Grand Condé, a famous general. They thought that Mazarin was attacking their power and wealth, and raised private armies, with which they occupied Paris. The King was forced to leave, and Mazarin twice fled across the border into Germany. There was widespread unrest and fighting, bringing misery to the country. By 1652, the nobles were discredited. They were obviously being selfish and asking for too much, and Parisians hated the Spanish troops which Condé had brought to occupy the capital. In 1652, the "princes of the blood" withdrew from the city and Louis re-entered in triumph. Happy crowds shouted greetings and some people even tried to kiss the King's shoes.

After the Frondes, Louis and Mazarin were settled in power more firmly than ever. The opponents of absolute monarchy had shown the emptiness and selfishness of their ideas. The French monarchy thus avoided the fate of the English. Louis himself learned hard lessons from the Civil War. He never again trusted the nobility, and refused to give them any real responsibility in the state during his reign. He also came to dislike the ordinary people, the *canaille*, as he called them, who, at one stage of the Frondes, had boldly pushed their way into his Palace bedroom to see him asleep. Louis was later to leave Paris permanently to

"There were terrible agitations in the state ... A prince of my blood and a very great name at the head of the armies of our foes; many parties of plotters in the state; the Parlement in possession of usurped authority; in my court little fidelity without personal interest ..." *Louis XIV on the Frondes, in "Memoirs".*

Below A symbolic statue showing Louis, again as a Roman general, triumphing over the Fronde.

19

make his court at Versailles, well away from the mob. Thirdly, he learned the danger of having an unpopular minister and resolved that he would rule alone when he came of age.

Meanwhile, from 1653 until his death in 1661, Mazarin wielded great power in France, further building up the machinery of government that would allow Louis to rule as a strong king. He was equally successful abroad. Two treaties with the Hapsburg powers, Spain and Austria, secured Richelieu's aims in foreign policy. The Treaty of Westphalia of 1648, which ended the Thirty Years War, gave France control of much of Alsace. It also ensured that Germany was still divided into over three hundred small states within the Holy Roman Empire, and so did not threaten France in the north-east. In 1659 the Treaty of the Pyrenees, concluded with Spain, strengthened France's frontiers in two weak spots by giving her the province of Roussillon, in the Pyrenees, and part of Artois, taken from the Spanish Netherlands. The Hapsburgs were now in decline; France's star was rising.

Below Louis, surrounded by bodyguards, passing the Louvre on his return to Paris after the Frondes.

5 The Rising Sun

IN JUNE 1654, FOLLOWING FRENCH TRADITION, Louis went to Rheims Cathedral to be crowned. During the complicated but splendid religious ceremonial, the fifteen-year-old king received the royal insignia, including the diamond ring that "wedded" him to France, and the crown, encrusted with diamonds and pearls. He was annointed with the holy oil that supposedly came "directly from Heaven." Dressed in his gorgeous robes, Louis appeared "in all his magnificence and with so majestic a bearing that he delighted the hearts of all beholders." Gold and silver coins were flung to the crowds, who pressed "to feast their eyes on the Sovereign on whom they could not gaze enough,

"Who does not admire the youth
Of a King more handsome than
   the day?
When he sings and dances,
The women sigh at the sight of
   him
And each blushingly admits
That it is well that he is not
   mature.
Anonymous Court poet on Louis, aged 15.

Below A tapestry showing Louis receiving ambassadors from the Pope in 1664.

and to express their joy by overwhelming him with cheers and blessings.'' As a new-crowned king, Louis' first public ceremony was strange: two thousand people, suffering from a disease called scrofula or "the King's evil,'' gathered to be touched by the monarch. This gesture and the words, ''The King touches thee, God heals thee,'' were supposed to bring rapid cure.

In training Louis for his future rôle, Mazarin played an important part. From the age of fourteen, the King had daily conferences with his godfather to discuss state affairs. Thus he learned his craft from an experienced statesman. He was introduced to Councils of State, which discussed all the problems involved in running the kingdom. The meetings were especially simplified for his benefit, and he was able to listen to discussions about foreign policy: how to maintain the balance of power in Europe, and whether or not to go to war; about colonial policy, which involved taking decisions about whether France should try to set up colonies, and if so, where; and about domestic policy, which was concerned with preserving the delicate balance of status and power between noblemen, town corporations, religious bodies and state officials. There were also detailed decisions to be taken, such as appointments to government posts. Louis thus had an early chance to test his judgment of men and policies. ''I was greatly pleased,'' he wrote in his *Memoirs*, ''when I discovered that my first thoughts were the same as those reached by able and experienced men.''

Mazarin's letters showed immense, almost fatherly, pride in Louis. He considered that he ''had the stuff for several great kings and one good man,'' that ''this will be a prince as accomplished as any that we have seen in several centuries.'' He continually encouraged Louis to live up to his promise: ''God has given you all the qualities for greatness; you must put them to use . . . When you are at the helm of state, you will do more in one day than one more clever than I could do in six months . . . I will die happy when I see you prepared to govern by yourself.''

Below and *right* Louis wearing two of the costumes he designed for ballets at court. Both display his favourite emblem, the sun.

Louis learned about war as a youth by campaigning with his troops under the great General, Turenne. He followed operations as a spectator during the fighting against the Spanish at Dunkirk and Mardyke in 1658. His handsome appearance impressed the troops. "One cannot tell with what joy and applause the troops received His Majesty," wrote Mazarin to the Queen-Mother. He shared the troops' rations and slept under canvas. He liked making out orders for the day, making up the secret passwords or inventing special trumpet fanfares. This love of detail remained in him all his life. From his mid-teens, Louis formed the habit of visiting his armies every spring.

One of his valets described a day in Louis' life at court when he was about sixteen. It was a life lived in public. The King awoke to prayers in bed and historical reading by a tutor. Important men were invited to his *lever* (getting-up ceremony), and as he dressed, he talked "in an easy affable manner that delighted them." Then he exercised vigorously in a simple gymnasium, where he "vaulted with wonderful agility" and drilled with a pike, or fenced. Having changed into formal clothes, he went to study state affairs with the Cardinal. Late in the morning, he attended the Queen's breakfast, and then went to Mass. In the afternoon he loved to hunt in the Bois de Boulogne. He was also a crack shot, and an expert falconer. Sometimes he would show himself in public on the Royal promenade by the Seine outside the Tuileries palace. His day was crowded with activity: "One cannot sufficiently admire the incessant activity of our young Monarch," commented *La Gazette*.

Evenings were spent at amusements: story telling, mimes, card-games for money, or playing *hoca*, a fore-runner of roulette. Louis grew to be a passionate gambler, like Mazarin and the Queen-Mother. Sometimes there were special entertainments, in which the King took part. He loved the ballet particularly, being a fine dancer. Scenes, such as the "Four Seasons" or "Pleasures of Town and Country," were presented as brilliant *tableaux* in magnificent costumes. Louis'

favourite rôle was Apollo, the Sun-God. He also danced as Bellona, Goddess of War, or as a Fury, his face covered by a terrifying mask. These rôles oddly anticipated the various faces he would one day show to Europe.

Louis' position dictated that he should marry someone of his royal rank, from one of the ruling families of Europe. His own romantic taste chose Marie Mancini, one of the *Mazarinettes*, nieces of his godfather, brought to court to find rich husbands. However, Louis knew his duty and agreed to the official choice of bride, Maria Teresa, daughter of Philip IV of Spain. The marriage, arranged as part of Mazarin's diplomatic negotiations, was to help seal the peace treaty of the Pyrenees in 1659. Maria was dull and uninspiring,

Right Maria Teresa, later Louis' wife, painted in 1652 by Diego Velasquez, the court painter to the King of Spain.

24

showing many of the defects of inbreeding in the Hapsburg family. The marriage was celebrated twice: once in Spain, by proxy, as for the sake of respectability the Infanta had to be married before she crossed the border; then at a second, more lavish ceremony in France on 6th June, 1660.

Louis and Maria made a triumphant entry into Paris. The Queen travelled in a golden coach, "that shone as brightly as the sun itself," through streets spread with fresh flowers and sweet-smelling herbs. The King was on horseback, "dressed in a costume, covered all over with silver lace, sewn with pearls and trimmed with pink ribbons, and a hat . . . whose splendid plumes were held in place by a diamond brooch." Even the mules in Mazarin's cavalcade wore harness of solid silver and plated gold.

Mazarin was already fatally ill. He had completed Richelieu's work by giving France a leading place in Europe, and saved the Bourbon throne from hostile rivals. He had also prepared Louis for his future rôle as a King with absolute power. His death in March 1661 appeared to his godson as "the greatest affliction I could experience." Louis XIV was left to rule alone.

Above Louis and Maria Teresa have their second, more splendid wedding ceremony in Le Mans cathedral.

"The Infanta Queen is small but well built; we admire the striking whiteness of her skin . . . Her blue eyes seemed to us beautiful; they charmed us by their softness and their brilliance. We recognized the beauty of her mouth; her lips, perhaps a bit too large, but still beautiful, also received our praise. To tell the truth, if her body were a little bigger and her teeth more beautiful, she would merit a place among the most beautiful women of Europe . . . But her costume was horrible: neither the cut nor the style pleased the eye.
Mme de Motteville on the Infanta Maria Teresa.

25

6 Personal Rule

LOUIS NOW ASTONISHED HIS COURT by deciding to take personal control of all state affairs. When officials asked him to whom they should apply about national business, he replied simply, "To me." He told his Secretaries of State: "Up to this moment I have been pleased to entrust the government of my affairs to the late Cardinal. It is now time that I govern them myself. You will assist me with your counsels when I ask for them . . . I order you not to sign anything, not even a passport . . . without my command." Although no previous king had insisted on such close personal control over the running of the government, nobody dared to disagree. At twenty-two, Louis now had the imposing appearance and commanding personality that seemed naturally to set the King apart from the other men: "agreeable personally . . . but with a lofty and serious air which impressed everyone with respect and awe, and prevented even his confidential advisers from forgetting his position when they engaged in private conversation with him."

There were various aspects of his rôle as King. He was first of all a soldier: war, which meant a chance for his followers to achieve wealth and fame, was expected from a seventeenth-century monarch. He was also a statesman and politician, running the administration of the state dealing with the changing forces that threatened it. Lastly he was a judge, settling disputes and giving justice. Louis shared besides the ideas of the English Stuart Kings that monarchs were divinely appointed to do God's work on Earth: "When God raised Kings to their thrones, He intended that they

> "I could almost feel my spirits and my courage rising. I was a different person. I discovered something new about myself and wondered joyfully how I could have ignored it for so long. That first shyness, which always comes with good sense and which was especially disturbing when I had to speak at some length in public, vanished in less than no time. I knew then that I was King, and born for it. I experienced an indescribable delight . . ." *Louis on becoming absolute ruler, 1661, in "Memoirs".*

> "Whoever takes the measure of the earth and me
> Will find the earth has far less majesty."
> *Lines from a court opera, describing Louis.*

should do their duty." He also hoped to restore the glory of the best of his royal ancestors. Finally he wanted to benefit all his subjects: "I wish to contribute by my efforts to the return of wealth, abundance and happiness of my people."

He set out his ideas on the duties of a King in his dictated *Memoirs*, written to instruct his eldest son. Four themes keep appearing in this work: "My dignity," "my glory," "my greatness," "my reputation" *La Gloire* was to be his "dominant and ruling passion." He preferred "a high reputation above all things, even life itself." At home, he wanted to win this reputation by restoring peace and prosperity; abroad, by impressing his might on all other European rulers.

If glory was his goal, his methods were more down-to-earth. He followed two principles: first, that "the function of Kings consists primarily of using good sense;" second, that a King should work very hard "to keep an eye on the whole earth . . . constantly learning the news of all the provinces and all the nations." Despising idleness, he worked at least six hours a day, a regular timetable of state work he was to follow for fifty-five years.

He tried to oversee almost every detail of national life. The French archives preserve thousands of documents all signed with the tall, shaky signature "Louis." Many of these papers related to Louis' work as a judge. Despite the hundreds of different legal codes working in various towns and provinces of France, he managed to provide firm justice in that age of violence. An Italian observer commented: "Justice is quick all over the Kingdom . . . they capture a criminal today and hang him tomorrow . . . that is why we see so much human flesh on the highways." Most harshly treated were men who offended the King personally. The offender was arrested by a *Lettre de cachet*, a royal order placing him in prison without trial. (The most unfortunate criminals were sent to be slaves on the galleys in the Mediterranean. Chained to their oars, ruthlessly whipped, their life was terrible. A prisoner who tried

> **"The Kings of France are so pleasing to God that He chose them to become His lieutenants upon Earth."** *André Duchesne, a clergyman, on the Divine Right of Kings.*

Overleaf From an early stage in his reign Louis began to take a keen interest in the cultural and scientific life of France. *Above left*, he is shown giving instructions for the building of a national observatory, and *below left*, he is inspecting the observatory after its completion. The sciences were not so distinct from each other then as now, and the observatory was used for medical and chemical as well as astronomical experiments. *Right*, Louis receives the key to the new hospital for old soldiers, Les Invalides, from its architect Jules Mansart, Royal Superintendent of Buildings, Arts and Manufactures.

LE ROY   MONSEIGNEUR   M.r Mansart
                                               Sur Intendant des Batimens

to escape might lose his ears or nose. The galleys were the labour camps of that age.) A network of spies and police kept Louis informed of dangerous men. They commonly opened people's letters to look for possible treason.

Louis struggled hard to do away with rivals to his power. He commented bitterly on the country in 1661: "Chaos reigned throughout." He was most angry with the Parlements for their part in the Frondes, and said that their "overweening arrogance . . . had put the whole realm in jeopardy during my minority . . . It was necessary to humble them . . ." The Parlements lost so much of their influence under Louis that a Minister could say in 1679, "Troubles with the Parlements are out of date. So much so that they are quite forgotten . . ." The King strengthened the network of thirty Intendants, his direct representatives in the provinces, and reduced the power of the nobles in local government. The Intendants supervised the collection of taxes and the administration of justice in their provinces, and kept the King informed about possible sources of trouble. Louis preferred to get his way with soft words, but was always ready to back them up with physical force. "A prince should first of all employ the means of gentleness and persuasion," he told his son. However, "it is certain that once it concerns either obstacles or rebellion, it is in the interests of a King's glory that he make himself obeyed." On several occasions, soldiers (including d'Artagnan and his musketeers, made famous by Alexandre Dumas' nineteenth-century novel) were sent to the provinces to crush revolts. "However bad a King may be," said Louis, "the revolt of his subjects is always criminal."

Personal rivals to power were quickly eliminated. The most famous was Nicholas Foquet, the dashing, handsome Superintendant of Finances in 1661. Foquet hoped to become First Minister. He gathered a party of supporters, and his fortified castle, Belle Isle, looked particularly dangerous to the King as the possible base for a new Fronde. Moreover, Foquet had stolen much

"He has an elevated, distinguished, proud, intrepid, agreeable air . . . a face that is at the same time sweet and majestic. His hair is the most beautiful in the world. His legs are handsome and well-made . . . he is the best-built man in the Kingdom. He dances divinely and loves ballet.

His manner is cold; he speaks little except to people with whom he is familiar . . . Then he speaks well and to the point. He jokes agreeably, and always in good taste . . . He properly acts out the role of King." *Anne Marie Louise, the King's cousin, describing Louis in 1660.*

money collected as taxes, and had built himself a lavish Château at Vaux, finer than any royal palace. Here he rashly invited Louis for a week of splendid entertainment. The King saw the magnificent grounds with a thousand fountains, and richly decorated rooms; he heard music by Lully, the best French musician, saw a play by Molière, the new star of French drama, and ate rich food prepared by the best cooks, served on gold plates. He resented this splendour which outdid his own. Foquet was arrested and imprisoned for life. Some say he became the famous Man in the Iron Mask, a mysterious prisoner about whose identity many fantastic stories were told. Louis' last rival was out of the way. Moreover, seeing the Château at Vaux prompted Louis to plan an even more splendid palace of his own.

Thereafter, the King ruled with the help of a small group of men that he could trust, following another of his guiding principles, to make "a careful choice of the persons who were to support and relieve me." Three men were outstanding: Jean Baptiste Colbert, Controller General of Finance; Michel le Tellier (and his son the Marquis of Louvois), Secretary for War; and Hughes de Lionne, Foreign Minister. They were all of middle-class origin, hard-working and anxious to please. With them, Louis embarked on reforms within France that would allow him to win glory abroad.

The two le Telliers, successively Ministers of War under Louis XIV; *left*, the father, and *right*, the son.

7 Money for War

LOUIS NEEDED MONEY to make possible the wars in which he could win the glory he dreamed of. In 1661 France's national finances were in a dreadful state. After the Spanish war and the chaos of the Frondes, the peasants were literally in danger of starvation. Many villages lay in ruins. The northern provinces were littered with the gaunt wrecks of more than eighty churches. All armies had stolen livestock for food; vines had been cut down; fields lay choked in weeds. Building, especially of workshops, was at a standstill. There was little trade. While the National Debt stood at £143 million, the King's income was a mere £72 million a year. The nation appeared almost bankrupt.

Louis' Minister, Colbert, seemed a dull, grey character to the court. His grim appearance, cold manner and austere way of life earned him the nickname "the North" or "the man of marble." His whole life was work. He did at least ten, sometimes fifteen, hours a day. His clear mind and zest for detail, his honesty and devotion to the King and the idea of France, soon earned him Louis' respect.

Colbert's ideal was to make France and its King rich by modernizing the French economy and by making people work harder. He looked enviously at the methods of the efficient Dutch, the richest people in Europe, whose wealth came from overseas trade and efficient, intensive farming. His first step was to reform the tax system. The French peasant and poor town worker had to pay several taxes. There was the *taille*, based on a man's income or the land he owned. Then there were taxes on certain products. The *aides* were

Opposite A symbolic representation showing Louis as a Roman emperor, with the help of the Greek heroes Perseus and Hercules, vanquishing the forces of evil in his second conquest of Franche Comté in 1674.

Below A marble bust of Jean Baptiste Colbert (1619–1683), Louis' chief minister.

levied on wines and spirits, and the *gabelle* on salt, which everyone was forced to buy in large quantities. Aristocrats and clergymen escaped these taxes. Colbert decided to reduce these burdens on the poor, while forcing the tax collectors, who stole two-thirds of what they gathered, to keep stricter accounts. By 1667, the King's income from taxes had doubled. In the same time, Colbert halved the costs of the King's court, despite grumbles from Louis, as lavish parties, new buildings and splendid clothes were part of his idea of glory. Colbert encouraged trade and industry. Foreign craftsmen were allowed to settle in France to teach their skills: German and Swedish experts in mines and metals; Dutch textile weavers and lace-makers; Venetian glass and mirror workers; Russian leather craftsmen; English goldsmiths and steel workers; German sugar refiners. A modest industrial revolution spread across France. Colbert's most famous act was the revival of French tapestry-making. The state-owned Gobelins workshops, in Paris, became the showpiece of French industry, famous throughout Europe. Paris became a new world centre of Art and Magnificence. A report from the Venetian Ambassador in 1668 said: "Whatever is best from every part of the world is now being manufactured in France." Hard work became a national mania. Colbert and his armies of clerks kept a very close eye on business activity, issuing minutely detailed rules for manufacture – for example the number of strands per inch to be used in weaving cloth.

Colbert also tried to make businessmen more respected. He advised the King "to receive with special marks of favour and protection all merchants who come to court." But snobbery still made the successful tradesman seek a title and give up his business to enter the "refined" world of the nobility.

Imports were discouraged by heavy tariffs on foreign goods. Trading companies, such as the Company of the East and the West India Company, were set up to compete with the merchants of Holland and England, and to form proper trade links with France's growing

overseas Empire: New France in Canada, fourteen West Indian islands, and Senegal and Madagascar in Africa. The colonies themselves were encouraged to grow, in size, wealth and population. French girls were "exported" to Canada as wives for settlers, and the parents of large families were rewarded by the King himself. It was difficult, though, to persuade the French to invest in trading companies; and apart from supplying a few luxuries such as sugar, the colonies had little influence on life in France.

Colbert also created a French Navy, although Louis showed little personal interest in war at sea. By 1671 France had a hundred warships, of the best designs, including the flagship *Le Grand Louis*, which was splendidly decorated with carved sea-horses and tritons, paintings and sculpture, ivory and ebony wood. The Navy was to protect the ever-growing merchant fleet.

Colbert's dream was of a hard-working, efficient state pouring money into the Treasury. He hoped that Louis and France could win glory and greatness simply through business activity. Louis did not share these views. He appreciated France's restored wealth, but for himself he valued only glory from war.

Above A tapestry, made at the Gobelins factory in Paris, showing Louis and Colbert inspecting the workshops there.

35

8 The New Army

"Flattery fed the desire for military glory that sometimes tore him from his loves . . . Louvois easily persuaded him that he was a better leader and strategist than any of his generals. All their praise he took with admirable complacency and truly believed that he was what they said. Hence his liking for reviews, which he carried to such lengths that he was known abroad as the 'Review King', and his preference for sieges, where he could make cheap displays of courage . . . He greatly enjoyed the sensation of being admired as he rode along the lines . . . He had a natural bent towards details and delighted in burying himself with such petty matters as the uniforms, equipment, drill and discipline of his troops . . . this enchanted his Ministers . . . managing great affairs of state in their own way whilst they watched him drowning amidst trivialities . . ."
The Duc de Saint-Simon on Louis the soldier.

ONLY SEVEN YEARS OF THE SEVENTEENTH CENTURY passed in complete peace in Europe. Wars were fought on an ever-increasing scale. Thanks to the reforms of his two Ministers of War, Le Tellier and Louvois, Louis XIV's Army became the most efficient and advanced of its time, until perpetual fighting bled France's strength into weakness.

The French armies of the Thirty Years War era had been, like most of those involved, mere gangs of tough, ill-paid soldiers, held together by some popular leader, enthusiastic only for the loot they gathered in ravaging friend and foe alike. Regiments were raised by great nobles, as they had been in medieval times. The King held no absolute power, being merely one of many leaders. Officers bought and sold their commissions for profit. Many were swindlers, claiming pay money for more men than there actually were in their companies. At the annual inspections they filled the ranks with *passe-volants*, beggars and servants. Discipline was kept only by flogging and hangings. Mass desertion was common. Many foreign soldiers fought in the French ranks: after a defeat, these might leave to seek richer plunder elsewhere.

Louis' reforming Ministers were father and son: the "supple, adroit, artful" Le Tellier shared power with his son, Louvois, violent and domineering, "the greatest bully imaginable." Louvois, the creator of the new French Army, was an expert in military matters but a disastrous influence on Louis by encouraging him to indulge his taste for war.

Reform began with the structure of the Army. The

King himself became Commander-in-Chief in 1661, and thereafter all officers obtained their commissions from him. A new, effective system of ranks was devised, and promotion could no longer be bought but had to be won by merit. The Army became "a career open to the talented;" Saint-Simon, the famous diarist, recalled an officer who "had started life as a swineherd, and had raised himself by sheer merit." The dregs of society were no longer good enough as recruits: a soldier had to be physically fit and under forty. Regular payment helped stem the tide of deserters. Uniforms (an idea introduced in Cromwell's New Model Army in England) were gradually adopted in France during Louis' time. Finally, soldiers' welfare was better cared for: the Hôtel des Invalides for poor ex-soldiers was opened in 1674.

Louvois insisted on strong discipline. The very word for a strict officer in the English Army is derived from the French Inspector of Infantry, Jean Martinet, who toured units hunting out inefficient officers. Those who cheated with "passe-volants" were severely punished by loss of rank and pay. Training for officer cadets, previously haphazard, was given in certain frontier towns, where they could see the army in action as well as studying technique.

In choice of weapons, Louvois was conservative. For the vital infantry fire-power, the up-to-date weapon was the *fusil*, a handgun fired by a flintlock. Louvois obstinately preferred the out-dated musket, fired by a slow, complicated technique. Once filled with ball and powder, it was raised to the shoulder, rested on a forked stick to aim, and fired by a slow match. It was not surprising that, in battle, the French threw away their muskets when they could find abandoned enemy fusils. The obsolete pike was still used to form the defensive "hedgehog," although the new, needle-shaped bayonet was appearing in battle. The cavalry, main attacking force of the period, was improved, with smaller horses and riders armed with sabres instead of swords. Cannon for siege operations were now brought under

Overleaf The entire court followed the army on its campaigns. Here Louis and Maria Teresa go in procession behind a large body of soldiers on their entry into Arras, on the border with the Spanish Netherlands, in 1667.

"At this period war really resembled a game of chess. On the field of operations, duly marked out and delimited, the Generals began the contest every year in spring. When, after complicated manoeuvres, one of the adversaries had lost or gained several pieces – towns or fortresses – the decisive battle took place: from the top of some slope, where the whole chessboard – the battlefield – lay before him, the Marshal moved his fine regiments backwards and forwards ... Check and Mate, the loser cleared his board: the pawns were put back into their boxes, or the regiments into their winter quarters, and each one went off to his private affairs while awaiting the next game."
J. Boulenger, "The Seventeenth Century in France".

Above A seventeenth century battle was often a scene of total chaos, and it was hard to tell which army was gaining the advantage. Here the French attack the Dutch at the battle of Senesse in 1674.

Army control – previously they had been hired to regiments by civilian contractors.

Louvois revolutionized army supply. His nickname was "the great victualler." Besides inventing a portable oven to bake bread on the march, he also set up dumps of food, fodder for horses, and ammunition. These were near the frontiers, and allowed his armies to start the campaigning season earlier, or to live in war-ravaged areas, sure of their supplies. The old idea of retiring into "winter quarters," followed since Roman times, began to die.

The French were lucky in Louis' time to have a genius in charge of military engineering. Sebastien Vauban had studied the art of fortification according to ancient Roman principles. So expert did he become

40

that it was said: "The town defended by Vauban is impregnable; the town invested [besieged] by Vauban is taken." His skill captured fifty towns in his career, with spectacular sieges carefully set out in stages over several weeks, "like the five acts of a tragedy." The King, sometimes even court ladies, came to watch the climax as if it were a play at the theatre; violins played sweetly as the town gave in. Vauban's forts were built at ground level, using complicated trench systems (still imitated years afterwards in the 1914–18 War) that allowed cunning defensive crossfire. Later in Louis' reign, Vauban designed a network of fort-resses along the northern frontier from Strasbourg to the North Sea. The forts gave France a defence in depth that protected her from invasion even after disastrous battle losses in Flanders in the first years of the next century. Vauban was never popular with the King, though, as he was a constant critic of the waste-fulness of the Court and the injustices in French society.

The French Army that took the field in Louis' first European Wars was the finest seen that century. Consisting of some 280,000 men by the 1680s, it was centralized, like the whole country, under the King's command. Only at the very end of his reign, when the great generals and ministers were dead, and France's resources exhausted, did this Army fail its King.

"His hair was tied with two, wide flame-red ribbons to match his flame-red high plumed hat. He wore a Venetian lace collar over a gorget of gold. His jerkin was of pale blue material, the blue almost hidden by gold and silver embroidery. Under the jerkin could be seen a knee-length coat of gold-brocade, fastened with gold braid, inlaid with diamonds. His sword-belt was secured by two gold lilies each set with a large diamond. He wore fine woollen knee breeches, garters of flame-red ribbon embroidered with gold, snuff coloured stockings, matching calf-skin shoes and enamelled spurs attached with gold buckles encrusted with diamonds." *Louis, aged 27, reviewing a military parade.*

Below A medal celebrating the completion of Vauban's fortifications at Verdun, in 1671, after its purchase from Charles II of England.

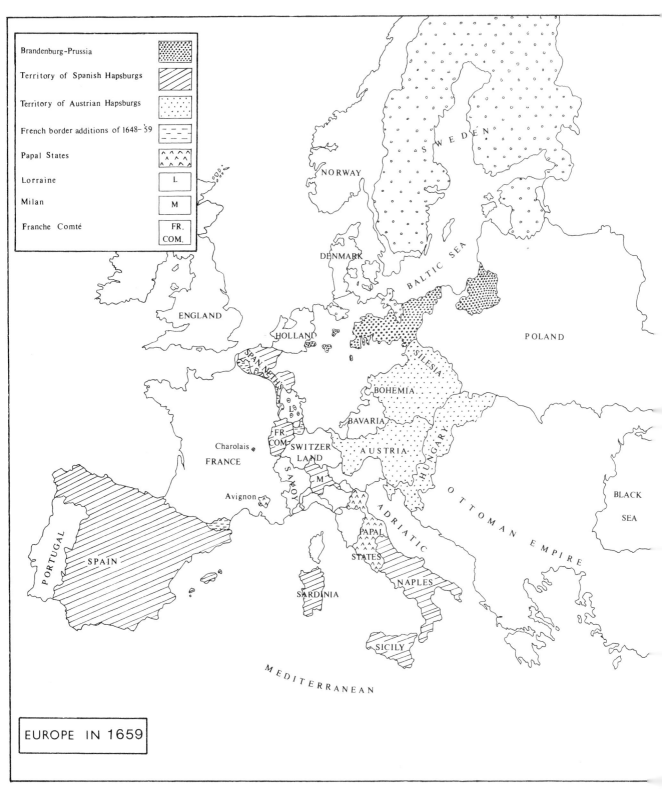

Brandenburg-Prussia	
Territory of Spanish Hapsburgs	
Territory of Austrian Hapsburgs	
French border additions of 1648–'59	
Papal States	
Lorraine	L
Milan	M
Franche Comté	FR. COM.

NORWAY

S W E D E N

DENMARK

BALTIC SEA

POLAND

ENGLAND

HOLLAND

SPAN. NETH.

SILESIA

BOHEMIA

BAVARIA

FR. COM.

SWITZER-LAND

AUSTRIA

HUNGARY

Charolais

FRANCE

SAVOY

M

Avignon

O T T O M A N   E M P I R E

BLACK SEA

ADRIATIC

PAPAL STATES

PORTUGAL

SPAIN

SARDINIA

NAPLES

SICILY

M E D I T E R R A N E A N

EUROPE IN 1659

9 First Flights of the Eagle

EUROPE, LOUIS WROTE, was "a vast arena that offered great opportunities for me to distinguish myself and to fulfil the great expectations that I had for some time inspired in the public." He dreamed of restoring the huge empire of his ancestor, Charlemagne, who "made the French name the terror of the whole earth." Charlemagne, the first Holy Roman Emperor, had ruled the greatest empire ever seen, and had won it, as Louis wrote, "by courage and by victories, which are the choice and the votes of Heaven itself when it has resolved to subordinate the other powers to a single one."

The French kings had for a long time seen the Hapsburgs of Spain and Austria as their particular rivals, and throughout the fifteenth and sixteenth centuries had fought repeated wars against them. The Holy Roman Emperor Charles V (1517–55) had ruled Spain, the Netherlands, Austria, Hungary and much of Germany, Italy and South America, and had dominated the civilized world in the same way that Louis had hoped to do. After Charles' death his empire was divided, and fell into decay. Austria's attention had been distracted from Western Europe by the attacks of the Ottoman Turks; Spanish power had declined because of a repressive domestic policy and repeated defeats in the religious wars that followed the Reformation, but had been propped up by the flood of gold and silver from Peru. Louis' grandfather, Henry IV, had won his throne by defeating the Spanish-paid armies of the Duke of Guise. Then, in 1643, the year of Louis' accession, France had won the battle of Rocroi against

> "A King need never be ashamed of seeking fame, for it is a good that must be ceaselessly and avidly desired, and which alone is better able to secure success of our arms than any other thing. Reputation is often more effective than the most powerful armies. All conquerors have gained more by reputation than by the sword." *Louis XIV, "Memoirs".*

Opposite The boundaries of the principal states of Western Europe after the Treaty of the Pyrenees in 1659, showing the territory in Flanders, Lorraine and the Pyrenees which France gained then or by the Treaty of Westphalia in 1648.

the Catholic German princes, who were supported by Spain and Austria. This battle brought to an end the Thirty Years' War, and, by the Treaty of Westphalia in 1648, the other nations of Europe accepted the terms dictated by Cardinal Mazarin.

Now, Leopold of Austria retained the impressive title of Holy Roman Emperor but had little real power over the hundreds of tiny German and Italian states which made up the Empire. Philip IV of Spain, "a skeleton proudly tricked out in glittering ornaments," watched the supply of precious metals from America dwindle to a trickle, and his influence in Europe evaporate with it. Louis, searching for glory, saw his chance of seizing some of the Hapsburg lands that still surrounded France like a decaying noose. In particular he wanted the Spanish Netherlands, which lay north of his country.

While his armies were prepared, Louis contented himself with certain shows of power, "first flights of the eagle" as they were called at the time. Ambassadors were then considered to represent the actual person of the King in foreign countries. When a quarrel broke out in London between the French and Spanish ambassadors as to who was more important, Louis was angry. Several Frenchmen had been killed in the fight. Louis threatened war, and the Spaniards gave in. Their envoy in France apologized to the whole French court. There was a similar clash with the Pope's soldiers in Rome. Louis ordered an army to march. Pope Alexander yielded, sent his nephew to apologize, and built a small pyramid in Rome as a monument to his regret. Louis also told his seamen not to salute the English ensign "on the English seas," as Charles II demanded. In such small incidents, Louis showed that he and France were to be respected.

Meanwhile Hughes de Lionne worked to isolate Spain in Europe by making alliances with other great powers. Diplomacy like this was a kind of war continued in peace-time. France allied herself with German Protestant states out of "zeal for German liberties," helped the King of Portugal against Spain, and won a Portuguese bride, with a large dowry, for Charles II of England. De Lionne also persuaded Charles to accept £400,000 for the port of Dunkirk, a bargain which Charles came to regret when pirates based there captured and plundered England's merchant ships during later wars.

Below A Gobelins tapestry showing Louis entering Dunkirk for the first time in 1662.

The first chance to gain real glory rather than petty triumphs of prestige came when French lawyers discovered that in Flanders there was an old law of "Devolution" by which children of a first marriage should inherit property before those of a second. This seemed to apply well to Louis' wife, Maria Teresa, daughter of Philip IV's first marriage. She could thus claim the Spanish Netherlands (Flanders) ahead of the Infante Charles, her stepbrother. Louis therefore had a "legal" argument for seizing these provinces.

In 1665 Philip IV died. There was no-one to help Spain; even the Holy Roman Emperor was busy fighting off Turkish invasion, and England and Holland were at war. Louis sent an army of 50,000 men into Flanders to seize what he claimed. Only two and a half months were needed for the French to capture the chain of Spanish fortresses: most of their defenders had been recalled to Spain. The Treaty of Aix-la-Chapelle in 1667 gave France large parts of the Spanish provinces and several fortresses. Louis' progress northward was watched fearfully by the Dutch, who saw their protective barrier dissolve. Although commercial rivalry had previously led them into repeated wars against the English, they now formed a Triple Alliance with England and Sweden "to curb the ambitions of France." This new combination persuaded Louis and his Portuguese allies to make a temporary peace with Spain.

Louis was now angry with the Dutch and determined to punish them. The Dutch United Provinces were Europe's newest state, having won full independence from Spain in 1648, though they had governed themselves since 1598. Much of the Dutch land lay below sea-level, reclaimed from the sea by drainage schemes of dykes and locks. Six small states clustered round the central state of Holland, whose "Grand Pensionary," John de Witt, led the Republic. The country had become rich by its mastery of the sea. Its ships carried most of Europe's trade. Its wealthy banks and exchanges at Amsterdam had replaced Genoa and Venice in Italy as centres of European business. The Dutch people, although great merchants, were also famous for their thrift. "They are the great masters of the Indian spices and of the Persian silks," wrote a contemporary, "but they wear plain woollen, and feed upon their own fish and roots."

Louis hated them for various reasons. Firstly they were a Republic, and had revolted against a king. To him, therefore, the Dutch were "a collection of maggots," governed by "businessmen and cheese merchants." Secondly, they had personally insulted him

Below A typical allegorical painting of the period showing Louis, attended by his ministers and watched over by classical gods and goddesses, declaring war against the Dutch.

in their newspapers. One cartoon, published after the formation of the Triple Alliance, showed a huge Dutch cheese eclipsing Louis' sun. Thirdly, they were Protestants, many of them extremist Calvinists, who did not allow Catholics to hold important offices in the Provinces. Fourthly, Louis was envious of their wealth. He was especially angry when they replied to Colbert's tariffs by imposing even heavier ones on French wine and brandy.

Louvois' aggressive ideas persuaded Louis to plan for war; for once, even Colbert was enthusiastic. Meanwhile Lionne had detached the Dutch from their allies: Charles II of England had been paid £166,000 in return for a secret treaty by which he promised to help France, and several German princes had signed similar agreements. In April 1672, Louis reviewed his powerful Army of over 100,000 men. Without a declaration of war, it swept northwards. Simple aggression lay behind this attack. It was the first of Louis' brutal acts that were to unite Europe against him.

The crossing of the Rhine was the first "victory" of the war. Louis' propagandist painters later showed this as a formidable feat, with the King himself leading the way. The river was, in fact, low and easy to ford; the

Below A Dutch medal shows the sun's rays losing their straightness as Louis, the "decrepit oppressor", destroys the Flemish town of Mons, while on the reverse William of Orange promises universal peace and prosperity.

resistance pitiful. Napoleon later laughed at this "triumph." Nevertheless, the French armies poured north through the undefended Spanish Netherlands towards Amsterdam. With heroic courage and determination, the Dutch broke their own dykes and flooded the land. Country houses, with their exotic gardens and famous tulip collections, and farms with their crops and animals, disappeared beneath the water. Amsterdam became a huge island fortress. Only certain raised roads remained, grimly defended, while small armed ships patrolled the waters. The French could not advance, even when winter froze the floods. They offered a peace, but demanded terms which the Dutch could not accept: loss of captured ground, a huge money payment, and equal rights for Catholics.

The Dutch now found a new leader to replace De Witt, torn to pieces by an angry mob during the French invasion. William of Orange (1650–1702) was descended from the famous William the Silent, who had led the struggle for Dutch freedom. He was already Captain-General of the Army, unimpressive to look at, but "a terrible man" in his determination to get revenge on Louis XIV. He was destined to become the French King's greatest European rival.

The entry of Spain and certain German states into the war in 1673 turned the fighting to France's eastern frontier. Franche-Comté was captured; Germany invaded. When the invasion of Holland failed the war had lost its purpose, and now it degenerated into random fighting. In 1674 England made a separate peace with the Dutch, and the war turned against Louis. His leading general, Turenne, was killed in battle. The war was costing £30 million a year, and suffering in France created local revolts. French efforts turned to diplomacy again, splitting her enemies so cleverly that, by 1678, France was able to win favourable terms at the Treaty of Nijmegen. She kept the Flanders fortress towns and Franche-Comté. The Dutch were exhausted, if not defeated. Louis' reputation now stood at its height: "He spoke to Europe as a master."

"The prince, a thin stripling, with bowed shoulders, a hooked nose between hollow cheeks, and a face seamed by small-pox, asthmatic, always ailing, carried in his frail body one of the most energetic souls that have ever existed . . . this terrible man, insensible to luxury, vanity, love, pity, pleasure, to everything save political passion, came very near to beating powerful France, and that Louis XIV whose opposite he was in every respect."
J. Boulenger, William of Orange.

10 The Sun King's Palace

COLBERT ALWAYS HOPED that the King's desire for glory would make him rebuild the Louvre Palace in Paris, perhaps even redesign the whole capital. "Nothing can add a greater glory to princes than buildings," he wrote. "All posterity will judge them by those great mansions which they have constructed in their lifetime." Louis agreed, but chose to build outside Paris, as he hated its filth and smells, and feared its mob.

His father had put up a small hunting lodge at Versailles, about ten miles south-west of Paris. In the first decade of his reign Louis had enjoyed coming here for special parties in the grounds. He decided to convert the "Little house of cards" into a Great Palace, which would be the supreme expression of his own glory. Having seen Foquet's Château at Vaux, he employed the same architect, Louis le Vau, and landscape gardener, Andre le Nôtre.

The park was set out as a vast formal garden. A great terrace led to pools and fountains with straight paths and avenues, making impressive vistas as they radiated into the surrounding woods. Lawns and flower beds (which blazed with colour even in winter as the flowers were changed each day) were cut into crisp, geometrical patterns. All was carefully balanced and ordered. Tiny temples and statues of classical gods stood where paths crossed. A mile-long grand canal was a key feature, with its hundred swans and its fleet of gondolas, miniature warships and yachts. To feed the thousands of fountains, pumps brought water from the Seine four miles away. Fully-grown trees were transported from all parts of France to make instant forests: in one year,

> "The place he designed for his magnificence in order to show by its adornment what a great King can do when he spares nothing to satisfy his wishes."
> *Mme de Motteville on Versailles.*

25,000 trees came from Artois province alone. The land was originally marshy, and scores of workmen, of the 36,000 on the site, died of malaria, their bodies being secretly transported away for burial by night. Particular features were the orangery, with twelve hundred trees growing indoors, and a zoo. Despite Louis' own pride in his gardens (he even wrote a guide book about them), they were always oppressive. As the Duc de Saint-Simon noted, "one admired and avoided them."

The Palace was impressive, if bleak and comfortless. In the centre were the Royal Apartments, with two wings housing the Princes and nobles. The King's own rooms typified the splendour of the decorations: their walls were faced with marble, although his study was lined with green velvet. It was a "palace of light," with large windows allowing light to reflect from gilded furniture and to illuminate glowing tapestries. The most spectacular room was the Hall of Mirrors, where, at night, the glassed walls reflected the thousands of candles. There were wonderful carpets, "big as meadows," and a painted ceiling showing scenes from Louis' victories, including "the unbelievable passage of the Rhine." Paintings and images of the King were everywhere, as was his symbol, the sun.

Nor was Versailles enough for the King. He built other smaller palaces in the Park – the Trianon, "a palace of marble, jasper and porphyry" for his ladies, and the superb small house of Marly, designed as his personal retreat from the Court. This was "a sumptuous and delightful abode" with its most beautiful gardens, but its cost made even Louis go pale when he saw the accounts.

Many critics have condemned Versailles as an expensive white elephant, revealing the madness for pomp and power that seemed to grip Louis in middle age. It was dangerous, too, because it cut the King off from his people. At the time, though, the Palace showed Europe "the splendid grandeur of the royal power," and was widely copied on a smaller scale by

Overleaf left Two views of the Palace of Versailles, *above*, as first built for Louis XIII, and *below*, as rebuilt by Louis le Vau. Notice the lines of guards in the front courtyard, and the number of people amusing themselves in various ways. On the *right*, two paintings of Louis with his family: *above*, a more fanciful version, showing them in classical Greek costume, by Nocret; *below*, a highly Realistic impression, by Largillière, of Louis with his son ("Monseigneur"), his grandchildren and the Duchess of Ventadour.

"The magnificence of the gardens is amazing but to make the smallest use of them is disagreeable . . . to reach any shade, one is forced to cross a vast, scorching expanse, and, after all, there is nothing to do in any direction but to go up and down a little hill, after which the gardens end. The broken stones on the paths burn one's feet, yet without them one would sink into sand or the blackest mud. Who could not help being repelled at the violences done to Nature?"
Saint-Simon on Versailles Gardens.

Left A panel in the ceiling of the Hall of Mirrors at Versailles, painted by Charles le Brun, commemorating the foundation of the Invalides hospital.

ambitious European princes, especially in Germany.

As further display of his magnificence, Louis made himself the leading patron of the arts, in a Golden Age of French culture. He instructed Colbert to draw up a list of poets, playwrights and scientists who were suitable to benefit from the royal bounty. This was in the hope that the artists he patronized would celebrate his glory. While Charles le Brun, Louis' court painter, designed flattering murals and statues to please the King, two of France's finest painters, Nicholas Poussin and Claude Lorrain, lived in Rome, preferring the freedom to paint as they chose to the stifling influence of royal charity.

Most of the famous writers of the age had some connection with the court. Many received pensions from the King, or sold the dedications of their works to prominent noblemen. The famous comedies of Molière were performed at Versailles, where courtiers delighted to identify certain characters with members of their own circle; and although Molière gently mocked the nobility, he was careful not to seem to attack the system. Racine's tragedies were much admired by the King himself, but, as Racine wrote to his son, it was his flattery rather than the quality of his writing that made him acceptable in polite society.

As Louis' wars became more expensive, he stopped spending so much on the arts, and the production of works in his honour declined. Some writers, amongst them noblemen, had always felt more free to criticize. In his "Characters" La Bruyère vividly described the peculiar strains and horrors of life at Louis' court. The *Fables* of La Fontaine and the *Maxims* of La Rochefoucauld provided biting comments on human life and behaviour, with some veiled references to the customs and follies of their own day. Madame de Sevigné and the Duc de Saint-Simon, both of them aristocrats, have left most accurate descriptions of the peculiarly formal society in which they lived, and of the state of France as a whole.

Louis delighted in music, above all, and his court musicians were given titles of nobility: Jean-Baptiste Lully and Francois Couperin wrote for the royal chapel and for concerts at Versailles, as well as teaching Louis' children to sing and play instruments. Although this age of artistic achievement had begun before Louis'

"Versailles, that most dismal and thankless of spots, without views, woods or water, without soil even, for all the surrounding land is quicksand and bog, and the air cannot be healthy . . . It diverted him to ride rough-shod over Nature and to use his money and ingenuity to subdue it to his will.
Beauty and ugliness, spaciousness and meanness were roughly tacked together. The Royal apartments at Versailles are beyond everything inconvenient, with back views over the privies and other dark, evil smelling places.
Versailles, that masterpiece where countless sums of money were thrown away . . . was so monstrously ill planned that it was never finished. Even the walls whose vast contours enclose a small province of the gloomiest, most wretched countryside, have never been completely finished." *Saint-Simon on Versailles.*

Seconde Journée
Concerts de musique sur une feuillée

Dies Secundus
Varij musicorum concentus sub frondea

> Je définis la cour un pays où les gens,
>
> Tristes, gais, prêts à tout, à tout indifférents,
>
> Sont ce qu'il plaît au prince, ou, s'ils ne peuvent l'être,
>
>   Tâchent au moins de le paroître.
>
> Peuple caméléon, peuple singe du maître;
>
> On diroit qu'un esprit anime mille corps:
>
> C'est bien là que les gens sont de simples ressorts.

Left A page from La Fontaine's *Fables*, showing the dying lion surrounded by flatterers, and in the verse attacking the hypocrisy of court life.

Opposite Two evenings of entertainment for the King and court at Versailles: *above*, a Greek tragedy set to music, performed in the courtyard of the palace, and *below*, a concert in the garden of the Trianon.

time (Foquet had been a notable patron), his lavish bounty to artists undoubtedly helped to make France the centre of European culture. Regrettably, towards the end of his reign, his intolerance and repression came to affect the arts too. The Academies of Art and Science, which Colbert had founded, became the means of imposing official standards on creative workers. "Important topics were forbidden," and art degenerated to become no more than entertainment or propaganda for the monarchy.

11 Life at Versailles

AFTER 1682, LOUIS BEGAN TO SPEND almost all his time at Versailles, gathering his family and courtiers around him. A strange special way of life developed.

The ritual of the King's day was the centre of the court. His every action was part of an elaborate ceremonial. He was awoken at eight. As musicians played outside his window, specially chosen courtiers gathered for the *lever*. Louis prayed (his rosary beads were each skull-shaped), washed in rose water and spirits of wine, and shaved every other day. After he had put on one of the large collection of royal wigs, the most privileged courtiers handed him his clothes: the Grand Master of the Wardrobe "would not have surrendered the honour of helping His Majesty pull on his breeches to any other being on earth." Now was the time for courtiers to ask special favours, such as appointment to official jobs which required little work but helped to support their expensive way of life. A cup of wine and a piece of white bread formed the King's breakfast, before the procession through the crowded state-rooms to attend Mass in the Chapel. Here everyone exchanged gossip during the service, while the King beat time to the music "with great elegance." The rest of the morning was spent on State work.

The King's mid-day meal was a popular public spectacle. A queue of humble citizens passed through the room as he ate, using his hands rather than a fork (then a novelty in Europe). Bowls filled with hot embers kept the food warm after its long journey from the kitchens. Afternoons were spent in hunting, which Louis loved to the end of his life, following his pack of

> "Give me an almanack and a watch, and I will tell you what the King is doing even if I am three hundred leagues away."
> *Saint-Simon, "Memoirs".*
>
> "Always the same pleasure, always at the same time and always with the same people."
> *Mme de la Fayette, a court lady, on the daily routine.*

Opposite The most famous and magnificent portrait of Louis, aged sixty-four, painted by Hyacinthe Rigaud just before his dreams of glory began to turn sour.

59

Above The gardens at Versailles, showing the crowds of courtiers who constantly thronged the palace (carefully posed by the painter).

Opposite A banquet given in 1687 by the leading citizens of Paris for Louis and his family, to celebrate the King's recovery from illness. Each diner is being served by a member of the city council. The smaller pictures show celebrations in provincial towns.

wolfhounds in a small carriage when he was too old to ride. Sometimes he simply walked in the grounds, his speed disconcerting his followers.

After more state business, the whole court gathered for the *appartements*, evening parties for dancing, acting, music, games and gambling. At ten, Louis dined with his family. He ate lavishly, one reported meal being four plates of rich soup, a pheasant, a partridge, ham and salad, mutton and garlic, pastries, fruit, and hard boiled eggs. (Even then Louis always had a "snack" of cold meats, loaves and bottles of wine at his bedside at night.) The King then retired with his famous bow to the company. His going to bed was another complicated ceremony, the *coucher*, at which more chosen courtiers, who paid heavily for the privilege, assisted with the

LE DINE DV ROY A L'HOTEL DE VILLE DE PARIS

royal nightshirt. The greatest honour of the day went to the man elected to hold the King's candlestick. Then the lights went out, and, by one o'clock, another Versailles day was over.

Versailles was not simply a royal palace. It was also a way of controlling the state. By attracting the nobles to his court, and making them dependent on him for money and advancement, Louis destroyed their power. All ambitious men were drawn to the palace. Once there, the costly show of court life and its ruinous gambling drained their money. The nobles no longer wanted to raise private armies from among their tenants and make themselves almost independent on their country estates. Indeed, the most dreaded punishment was exile to the provinces. One man told the King on his return to favour, "Sire, far from your presence a man is not only unhappy, he is ridiculous." Thus the Intendants were free to govern France in the way that Louis wanted it governed.

Accommodation at Versailles was often only "two small, dark garret rooms, into which neither light nor air could penetrate." Even these were only won after long intrigue. Less fortunate beings were lodged in the town that grew up beside the Palace.

The courtier had to be up at dawn, preparing his elaborate clothes for the *lever* of the King. He joined the crowd in the state rooms hoping for a glimpse of Louis, perhaps even a word or a nod from him. A mild royal comment on the weather could save a man from his creditors for six months. The day was spent amid the splendour of the Palace rooms, in "the terrible heat" and "infernal noise" that Saint-Simon said made life there so tiring and uncomfortable. The men discussed horses and hunting, or the chances of royal favour; the women exchanged court gossip. The public, too, could enter the Palace, and beggars and .hucksters were found on the staircases. Thefts were common.

For the new courtier, the code of court behaviour, its *etiquette*, caused great problems. There were many little tricks to learn. Within the Palace, you did not knock at

"The Court does not make a man happy; it prevents him from being happy elsewhere."
"It is hard to accustom oneself to a life that takes place in a waiting-room, in courtyards or on a staircase."
"A nobleman who lives at home in the country is free, but unsupported; if he lives at Court, he is protected, but a slave."
"Many men drag out their lives at Court embracing and congratulating those who receive favours, and die there at last, having gained nothing."
La Bruyère on Court Life, in "Characters".

Opposite A modern photograph of Louis' bedroom at Versailles. The palace is now preserved as a museum.

a door, but scratched it, growing one long fingernail especially for the purpose. In town, however, you knocked, a certain number of times according to the rank of the person visited. If you passed the King's dinner on its way to his table, you swept off your hat, bowed and murmured, "The King's Meal?" You raised your hat to ladies, more and more elaborately according to their rank.

The nightmare of etiquette was complicated by "precedence." The exact order of importance of people at Court caused endless difficulties. The King appeared to know exactly who came where, and was darkly offended if anyone took a wrong place. At every court ceremony or important marriage or funeral, the "rumbling volcano" of precedence was heard. The biggest battle centred on the "Three Chairs," the arm-chair, the armless chair and the stool. Who should have which? Before any big meeting of important people, messengers were sent ahead to discover the seating arrangements. Who could sit down in whose presence? Who was entitled to have both leaves of the door thrown open on a visit, and who only one? Lesser mortals received messages from their superiors standing up and hatless. Only at the evening *appartements* were the rules relaxed. Here the courtier was free to lose his money in comfort, before retiring to his garret for the night.

In this way, and in the pathetic search for honours, the courtiers' energies were absorbed. By this fantastic daily ritual, the King permanently destroyed the last powers of the nobility.

"The Courtier wears the finest of materials, but their magnificent quality is further enhanced by embroidery and decoration. If you ask him the time, he pulls out a watch which is a masterpiece; his sword handle is carved in agate; he wears on his finger a great diamond, an eye-dazzler, quite perfect; he lacks none of these odd playthings, worn as much out of vanity as because they are fashionable. He has a glittering equipage, drawn by six horses and followed by a great crowd of idle good-for-nothings."
La Bruyère describing the fashionable courtier.

12 Matters of Religion

AS THE KING GREW OLDER, his religious outlook changed considerably. His faith, learned from his mother, had always been simple and unquestioning. He had been careful to attend daily services and to say his prayers, yet remained unconcerned about his open sins. For example, he had had several mistresses, including the beautiful Louise de la Vallière and Madame de Montespan, by whom he had several illegitimate children.

Below Louis, in the presence of Maria Teresa, offers a pair of bracelets to his future mistress Louise de la Vallière.

A critic described him as "concerned for trifles; unfeeling towards terrible evils."

After Queen Maria Teresa's death in 1683, Louis turned his attention seriously towards religion. This was partly due to the influence of his second wife, Madame de Maintenon, whom he married in secret. She was pious, intelligent, older than Louis. The nobles at court were surprised by his choice. They considered Maintenon "an old frump," who seemed more suitable to be a governess than a royal wife. But Louis was faithful to her, as he had rarely been to Maria Teresa.

The King's religious policy was strangely contradictory. On the one hand, although he was a Catholic, he opposed the authority of the Pope over the French church; on the other hand, Louis hated "heretics;" anyone who did not accept the Catholic faith.

The clash with the Pope happened because of Louis' own concept of himself as a ruler appointed by God. His bishops supported his view: "Kings depend upon God and recognize no power above them." Louis wanted a Gallican or semi-independent French Catholic church, with himself in control of its practical affairs – very much like what Henry VIII had achieved in England in the previous century. He therefore carried on a continual battle with the Pope on the question of the *régale*. This meant that when a French bishop died, the King took the money income from his district, and appointed his successor. The quarrel about this privilege dragged on until more than thirty bishoprics lay vacant, and was only settled by a compromise granting Louis wider rights, after the Pope had been impressed by the King's vigour in suppressing the French Protestant "heretics," the Huguenots.

Louis's new piety led him to look again at the Huguenots, and the rights which his grandfather, Henry IV, had granted them by the Edict of Nantes of 1598. Although the Huguenots had lost some of their freedom under Richelieu, there were still about a million of them in 1680. They had local self-government in certain towns, and enjoyed great success as mer-

Above Madame de Maintenon, Louis' second wife, with her niece. She is wearing mourning for her first husband, the satirical poet Paul Scarron.

"The King is beginning to think seriously of his salvation. If God preserves his life, there will soon be only one religion in his Kingdom." *Mme de Maintenon, 1681.*

Above A Protestant cartoon shows Louis in a monk's habit, but with devil's horns on his head. The verse below reads: "The power of my sun brings heresy to light. It blows away the fogs of Protestantism, not because of holy zeal, but in order to hide my underhand political motives."

"To purge the state of an
    internal pestilence
Louis saw that it was time to
    cut its roots.
He broke the Edicts by which
    our recent Kings
Allowed this serpent the right
    to speak,
From which never ceased to
    come its false maxim
Infecting minds and fomenting
    crimes . . ."
Le Clerc, poem on the Revocation of the Edict of Nantes.

chants and tradesmen. Louis disliked the idea of a "state within a state." He remembered the old coronation oath of French Kings: "I will seriously endeavour to rid my land of heretics." He hoped to win Divine favour by carrying out this promise. His bishops were enthusiastic. Many of his subjects were jealous of Huguenot success.

From 1680 to 1684, the Huguenots were systematically attacked to make them change their faith: first by missionaries sent to preach to them; secondly by refusing to let them hold public offices or enter professions; thirdly by offering tax relief to converts to Catholicism. Then Catholics were encouraged to attack Protestant churches, and many were destroyed. The Huguenots were no longer allowed to run their own schools. Even births and deaths had to be assisted by Catholics, ready to snatch Protestant souls from the flames of hell. Worst of all were the *dragonnades*, forcible billeting of French soldiers in Huguenot houses. The troops could behave as they pleased, bullying the Huguenots into changing their faith. There were horrible tortures: people were thrown on fires or attacked by dogs, threatened with the bayonet, dragged to Mass by the hair and there sprinkled with Holy Water. Not surprisingly, many Huguenots were converted or pretended that they had been. Protestant opinion abroad was shocked. The English diarist, John Evelyn, wrote: "The French persecution of the Protestants, raging with the utmost barbarity, seems to exceed even what the heathen used."

By 1685, Louis was able to claim that the Edict of Nantes was no longer necessary, as there were so few Huguenots left. It was therefore cancelled by royal proclamation, and the Huguenots lost their remaining liberties. All Protestant churches and schools were closed. The dragonnades were enforced more brutally than ever. Ministers caught giving Protestant services were executed. Those attempting to escape from France were sent to the galleys.

Fortunately, the borders of France were too long to

guard completely. The Huguenots got away somehow, crossing the Alps or Pyrenees on foot, sailing in open boats across the Channel, hidden inside bales of goods, disguised as priests, or simply by killing frontier guards. They left in their thousands, taking their skills and their money to foreign countries, which were commercial rivals of France. They went to Holland, England, America and the German states, where they were warmly welcomed. Colbert's new industries were ruined. Most of the refugees were townsmen: bankers, merchants, skilled workers, doctors, and lawyers. Nine thousand sailors, six hundred army officers and twelve hundred soldiers also left, weakening Louis' forces as he stood on the verge of more, larger-scale wars. The King himself, wrapped in vanity, seemed indifferent to this devastating loss, merely commenting: "My realm is being purged of bad and troublesome subjects." Such were the results of Louis' conversion to a more pious way of life.

"The revocation of the Edict of Nantes, decided upon without the least excuse of any need . . . constituted a terrible plot which depopulated one quarter of the Kingdom, destroyed its commerce, caused widespread pillage and condoned the dragonnades, allowed torture and torments, in which many innocent persons of both sexes died by thousands; . . . caused our manufacturers to move abroad, where they flourished and brought wealth to other states . . . and gave them the spectacle of so remarkable a people . . . exiled, made to wander over the face of the earth, without being guilty of any crime, seeking shelter from their own country." *Saint-Simon, "Memoirs".*

"It is a work worthy of your reign. Through you heresy is no more; God along has performed this miracle." *Archbishop Bossuet on the Revocation of the Edict of Nantes.*

Left A secret Huguenot service in the mountains near Nimes.

13 The Warrior King

EVEN BY THE STANDARDS OF HIS TIME, Louis now began to appear as nothing more than an aggressive tyrant in his conduct of foreign affairs. In the seventeenth century it was still widely accepted that a king should be warlike. His princes and noblemen favoured war as a chance of winning fame, wealth and women. A lady of the Royal Family, la Grande Mademoiselle, spoke for women of her class when she said that she "adored" war and soldiers. The opinion of merchants and town officials, who preferred peace so they could carry on trade, was disregarded; nor did the feelings of peasants and workers who feared the devastation caused by armies of friend or foe, or those of the clergy, who dreamed of turning the King's warlike energies against the heathen Turk in a new crusade, carry much weight. Colbert's theories of "power through wealth," whereby France would become great through industry, trade and colonial expansion, were ahead of his time. In the 1680s Louis was increasingly influenced by men of violence, Louvois and Croissy, who told him that force alone would command respect. These "experts" became more and more obsessed with the problem of giving France secure frontiers. Royal finances were running out, but Louis continued to engage in ever more costly wars, until even his closest supporters were sickened by the waste and violence.

His first plan after the Treaty of Nijmegen was to make small gains of territory wherever he could. The Mediterranean and the Pyrenees in the south, the Atlantic in the west, the Alps in the south-east and Vauban's forts in the north meant that most of France

Opposite Louis painted as a Roman emperor, attended by a negro slave.

"Here ended the apogee of this reign and the heights of Louis XIV's glory and prosperity. The great captains, the great ministers at home and abroad were no more. Their places were taken only by pupils. We were now entering the secondary age . . . very different from the first." *Saint-Simon on 1688.*

71

> "In his walk, his speech, his countenance, in his whole person, there was an air of grandeur, a noble and imposing character, which came from the opinions he had formed of an absolute King, like the Olympian Jupiter shaking the universe with his frown. His face was correctly beautiful in spite of his age. One could have believed he was always on the point of speaking, and this gave the more value to his rare words, measured and weighed in the balance. His figure had been admirable, but the flesh which he put on in his devout days was beginning to mar the perfection of his contours. He even became too fat . . ." *Cardinal Dubois describing Louis in middle age.*

was secure against invasion. The obvious weakness was in the north-east, where the river Rhine, a hundred miles east of the French border, would have been the ideal frontier. There was also real confusion about the ownership of certain city fortresses in Alsace, along the Rhine. Louis' lawyers hunted out ancient chests full of title deeds, waterstained and chewed by rats. These were examined at special courts, the *Chambres de Réunion*. By this half-legal policy, Louis seized several towns in Alsace. Finally, by sheer force, he took Strasbourg, its capital and a major bridgehead on the Rhine. His army continued to nibble pieces from Imperial territory, and his fleet bombarded Genoa in Italy. No-one seemed able to resist. The Emperor was still away fighting the Turks. The Spaniards declared war half-heartedly, but lost further ground in Flanders and Luxembourg. The Truce of Ratisbon in 1684 left Louis with his gains after this policy of "gnawing and encroaching."

This French aggression caused great disquiet among her neighbours. The French King seemed to think "he is as much above other crowns as the King is above ordinary men." All Protestant countries were disgusted by the barbarous treatment of the Huguenots following the revocation of the Edict of Nantes. With

Below A Dutch cartoon of 1695 suggests that Louis' domination of Europe will be ended by the Dutch recapture of Casal and Namur.

the fall of Strasbourg, "a door through which France can invade German soil as often as she wishes," all the Empire seemed threatened. The great monument in the Place des Victoires in Paris offended the whole of Europe: it showed Louis the Great trampling the three-headed monster, the Triple Alliance, underfoot, while Germany knelt at his feet and Sweden was a mere slave in chains. Finally in 1686, after France had claimed the Palatinate, a German state next to Alsace, Louis' rivals drew together in an alliance against him. The League of Augsburg consisted of Austria, Spain, Sweden, several German states, Holland and England. When Louis' deadly rival, William of Orange, became King of England following the "Glorious Revolution" of 1688, France seemed alone against Europe.

Louis was not discouraged by the strength of the forces opposing him. In 1688 he invaded western Germany, seizing Cologne and the Palatinate. He had hoped that his enemies would be occupied elsewhere. Instead they rapidly formed up against him. The War of the League of Augsburg went on until 1697, fought on land and sea, mostly as siege and counter siege in Flanders and Italy, even spreading to the American colonies. Although both sides had heavier fire-power than before and large numbers of soldiers were killed, the fighting was inconclusive. It is best remembered for the notorious brutal devastation of the Palatinate by Louis' armies. It was Louvois' idea to destroy the whole area so that German armies could not advance across it. Houses were pulled down and set alight, vineyards and crops burned, bridges smashed, castles, even whole towns, laid waste. The people themselves were killed or forced to leave their homes. "All the roads are covered with carts," wrote an eye-witness, "and with terror-stricken families escaping they knew not whither." Years later, the Duc de Saint-Simon saw a wrecked town where the survivors were "burrowing under the ruins or living in cellars." These atrocities were among the worst of the violent seventeenth century, almost as bad as the terrible sieges of the Thirty

Above Louis meets the former James II of England *(left)* after he had been forced to abdicate by the "Glorious Revolution" of 1688. In the bedroom behind, the ex-Queen of England talks to Madame de Maintenon.

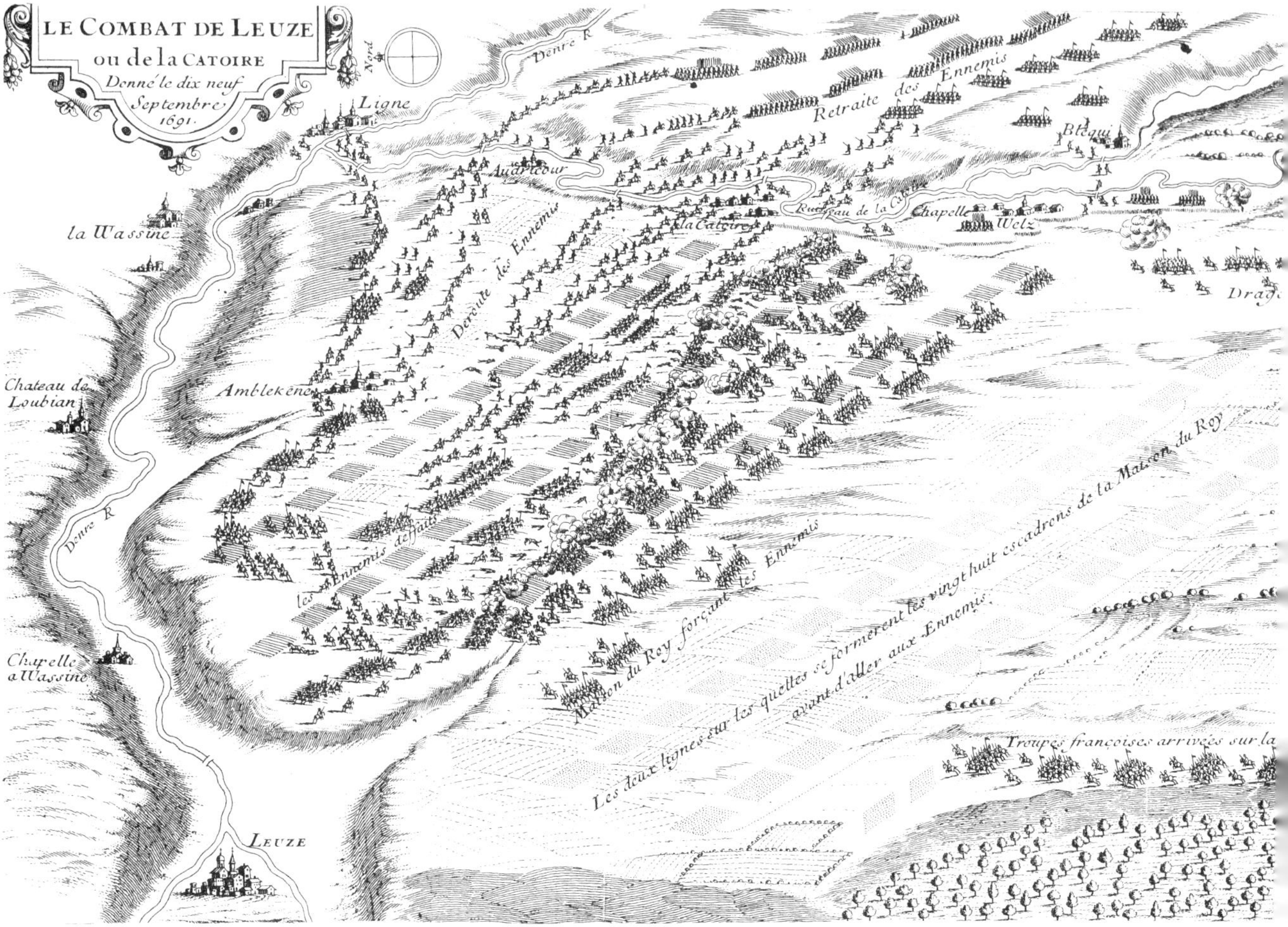
LE COMBAT DE LEUZE
ou de la CATOIRE
Donné le dix neuf
Septembre
1691.
Nord
Denre R.
Ligne
Retraite des Ennemis
Blequi
la Wassine
Ruisseau de la Catoire
Chapelle
Welz
la Catoire
Deroute des Ennemis
Chateau de
Loubian
Amblekene
Denre R.
les Ennemis deffaits
Maison du Roy forçant les Ennemis
Les deux lignes sur les quelles se formerent les vingt huit escadrons de la Maison du Roy
avant d'aller aux Ennemis
Chapelle
a Wassine
Troupes françoises arrivées sur la
LEUZE

Above A plan of the battle of Leuze, in 1691, showing the small units of cavalry with which the French were able to launch rapid attacks against less mobile enemies.

Years War. "The French are cannibals," said a German in a pamphlet.

It was a war of "many famous victories but few solid advantages." One of its famous battles was fought at the River Boyne in Ireland in 1690 where the dethroned James II of England, backed by French troops, was defeated by William of Orange, who was now King of England. War-weariness on all sides led to the Treaty of Ryswick in 1697. France lost Lorraine and several Flemish fortresses, and was on the point of giving up all the gains of the "gnawing peace" that had followed the Dutch War. Then, while talks about peace still went on, Louis' armies seized Barcelona, and, by using it as a bargaining counter, France was able to keep Alsace and Strasbourg.

France had proved she could still score dramatic victories, but Louis could not defeat the rest of Europe combined against him. He was forced to recognize William of Orange as King of England, and to stop supporting James II. Although Louis wrote of "the happy success with which Heaven has favoured my arms in the course of this long war," although firework displays at Versailles blazed the theme "Louis XIV gives peace to Europe," the King had to realize that his arch-rival had humbled him.

"There never lived a man more naturally polite . . . on no occasion did the King let slip an uncivil word to anyone. If he had need to rebuke, correct or reprimand anyone . . . it was done with a show, more or less, of kindness, seldom sharply, never angrily. Above all, he was unrivalled in his courtesy to women, for he never passed a petticoat without raising his hat, even when it was only a housemaid. He was punctual to the minute, and absolutely clear in his orders. He was sometimes gay but never undignified, and never at any time did he do anything improper or indiscreet. His smallest gesture, his walk, bearing and expression were all perfectly becoming, modest, noble and stately . . . His mind, which had a natural tendency towards small things, found pleasure in every kind of detail. He was the great ruler of the very small." *Saint-Simon, "Memoirs".*

Left The proclamation of the Treaty of Ryswick of 1697 in the courtyard of the Palace of the Tuileries. The treaty led to a brief spell of peace between France, Holland and England.

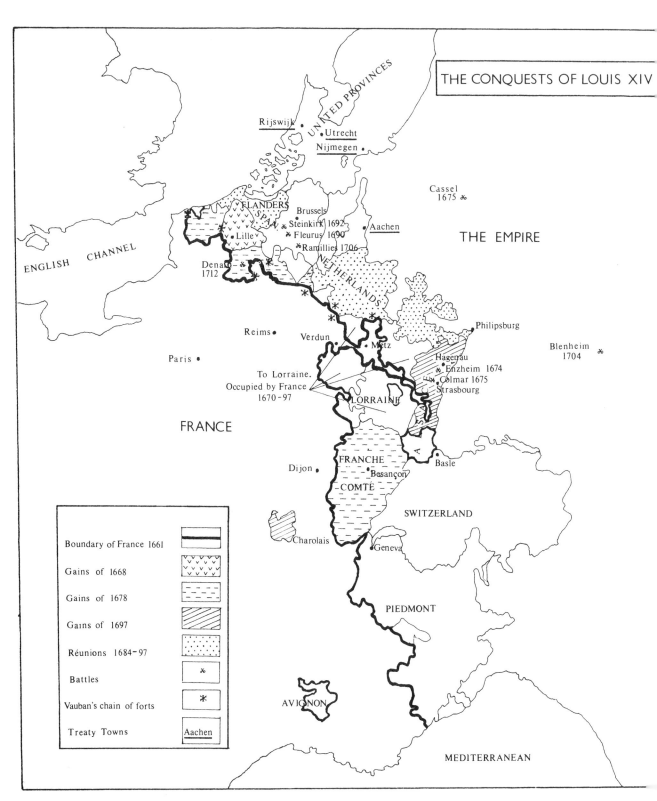

THE CONQUESTS OF LOUIS XIV

Rijswijk

UNITED PROVINCES

Utrecht

Nijmegen

Cassel
1675 ✱

FLANDERS
SPAIN

Brussels

Steinkirk 1692
✱ Fleurus 1690

Aachen

THE EMPIRE

Lille

Ramillies 1706

NETHERLANDS

Denain
1712

ENGLISH CHANNEL

Philipsburg

Reims

Verdun

Metz

Blenheim
1704 ✱

Paris

Hagenau
✱ Enzheim 1674
Colmar 1675
Strasbourg

To Lorraine.
Occupied by France
1670-97

LORRAINE

FRANCE

Dijon

FRANCHE
Besançon
COMTÉ

Basle

SWITZERLAND

Charolais

Geneva

PIEDMONT

AVIGNON

MEDITERRANEAN

Boundary of France 1661

Gains of 1668

Gains of 1678

Gains of 1697

Réunions 1684-97

Battles   ✱

Vauban's chain of forts   ✱

Treaty Towns   Aachen

14 The Spanish Succession

ONE FINAL DISASTROUS WAR was to mark the last years of Louis XIV's reign. Ever since 1665, when Philip IV, King of Spain, had died, leaving a sickly heir, Charles II, Europe had been wondering who would eventually succeed to the throne of the Spanish Empire. Charles was a wretched human being, full of inherited disease and inbred weakness. He could not read; he was able to walk only when held up by leather straps; he could not concentrate on anything difficult and spent the day playing with his court dwarves. Yet he somehow survived, even married, but did not produce an heir. Spain's huge, decaying Empire, guarded only by ragged soldiers, with its twenty crowns and remnants of American wealth, waited to be torn apart by other European powers.

There were various claimants through daughters of the Spanish Kings – girls who had married elsewhere in Europe. The most important were those in the French Bourbon family, through Maria Teresa and Anne of Austria, Philip IV's sister. The Emperor Leopold could also claim through his wife and mother, younger sisters of the Bourbon Queens. All European statesmen realized that if either France or the Empire took over Spain, the balance of power would be upset. There were, therefore, various Partition treaties signed between France, England and Holland, while they waited for Charles to die. However, the Spaniards decided to offer their crown to Louis XIV's grandson, who had been named as heir in Charles II's will.

When Charles finally expired in November 1700, Louis made a fateful choice: he abandoned the Parti-

"Contrary to all precedent, the King caused the two folds of the door of his cabinet to be thrown open, and ordered all the crowd assembled without to enter; then, glancing majestically over the numerous company: 'Gentlemen,' said he, indicating the Duc d'Anjou, 'This is the King of Spain. His birth has called him to the throne and also the deceased King by his will. The whole nation desired his succession and urged me to approve it: it was the will of Heaven. I agreed with pleasure.' Then, turning to his grandson: 'Be a good Spaniard. This is now your first duty, but remember that you were born a Frenchman to promote union between the two nations. This is the way to make them happy and to preserve the peace of Europe.'"
Saint-Simon on the new King of Spain, 1700.

Above A French cartoon of the Duke of Marlborough.

tion treaties and accepted the Spanish throne for his grandson, a boy of seventeen, who was proclaimed Philip V. Then, instead of reassuring his Partition allies, Holland and England, he stumbled into war with them by ill-judged decisions. Firstly he declared that his grandson could still inherit the French throne (thus uniting France with Spain); secondly, he sent troops to take key forts in Flanders – Mons, Luxemburg, Antwerp, Ostend – claiming them "in the name of Spain" and imprisoning the Dutch defenders who had occupied them since the Peace of Ryswick; thirdly he recognized the heirs of James II, the former English King, then dying in exile at Louis' court. In retaliation, the important European powers again united as the Grand Alliance (1701). Soon war once more blazed across Europe.

Although Louis's old enemy, William III of England, died in 1702, he was faced by a formidable new opponent: John Churchill, Duke of Marlborough (1650–1722). Marlborough was a brilliant soldier and diplomat, who, with the help of his wife and the Whig party in Parliament, dominated the court of Queen Anne of England (1665–1714). The Empire, too, had a great general in Prince Eugene, who had finally reversed the advance of the Turks into Europe and in 1699 had brought Hungary and Transylvania under Austrian rule.

The war went badly for Louis. His armies were outnumbered and now had to protect Spain as well. His most able generals were dead; state funds had been run down and his soldiers were still worn from the last war. In Italy, the French were quickly forced back to their frontiers. A French thrust into Germany aimed at the heart of the Empire was at first successful, but ended in disaster at the Battle of Blenheim in 1704. Here France lost her place as military leader of Europe, and Marlborough drove the French armies out of Germany. In Spain, the new King, Philip V, was threatened by an Imperial Army, headed by the Archduke Charles, heir to the Emperor, who also claimed the Spanish throne.

78

The English captured Gibraltar, opening the Mediterranean to their ships, while the Imperial Army seized large parts of Spain, until stopped by a French victory at Almanza (1707). Once again Flanders became the crucial battle-ground. Here Marlborough triumphed over the French at Ramillies (1706) and Oudenarde (1708). Only the caution of the Dutch and Vauban's chain of forts prevented Marlborough from invading France itself. A total eclipse of the sun observed in Europe in 1706 seemed to many to be a symbol of the declining fortunes of Louis XIV.

Below An engraving from an eighteenth century history book shows a heroic English trooper chopping a terrified Frenchman down from his horse at the Battle of Blenheim.

At home in France, attempts to find more money became desperate. New taxes were invented to squeeze more from the peasants. Although Louis had to keep up his usual appearance to impress his enemies, there was austerity at his Palace at Marly. The court became sombre. At meals, the guests sat "in the silence of the refectory of a convent; no one dreamed of talking or laughing." War news was nervously awaited. Courtiers became alarmed at the worry in each other's faces. Prayers were continually offered. If a horse galloped

Below A Dutch cartoon shows Louis, ill in bed, being comforted by the Devil and three of his mistresses; the Dauphin is about to stab him through the curtain, and a soldier crippled in his wars hobbles away cursing him.

past, courtiers rushed to the window, such was the tension at the Palace.

The nightmare winter of 1709 was another blow at France's fortunes. A three-month spell of stunning cold did massive damage. Rivers froze to their mouths and the sea along the channel coast was coated with ice, thick enough to support heavy carts. Birds and animals froze in the fields: France lost half its livestock. Travellers died of cold on the road. "The common people are dying like flies," wrote Madame de Maintenon. Most of the babies born at that time died. Corn and seeds were killed in the ground, vines and trees perished in the frost. Wolves wandered in from the forests to attack villages. As corn became scarce prices rose, causing rioting. People began to eat boiled grass, roots and the bark of trees.

The King was forced to stay indoors. His fires, in the huge draughty rooms of his Palaces, ate up whole forests of trees. Wine and water, freezing, broke their bottles on the table. Ink froze on the pen. Loaves of bread solidified during the meal. There was even a hunger march to Versailles from Paris, and, for the first time since the Frondes, Louis heard the shouting of the mob. Soon the Royal Family hardly dared show themselves. The courtiers, whose income depended on farming, were hardly better off than the peasants. Even the Army, it was said, had begun to sell their weapons to buy food. The following spring proved grim and sterile: "The earth seems dead," wrote a bishop at court. "It promises neither fruit nor yield. The King will soon be reigning over ghosts, and his country will be one vast cemetery."

These natural disasters, echoing the military defeats, seemed proof to Louis that God was angry with him. Yet he would not give in to the humiliating peace terms offered by the Grand Alliance in 1709, and his proud letter sent out to his people restored public morale slightly. France fought on. At Malplaquet, in September 1709, the French army under a new commander, Marshal Villars (1653–1734), killed 20,000 of

"Grand-dad is a braggart,
An imbecile the son,
Grandson is a coward vile,
Beauties everyone.
I pity all you Frenchmen
Who bend beneath their yoke.
Do as the English did, my
    friends –
And break it – at a stroke."
Paris street rhyme against Louis XIV.

"Our father which art at Versailles, Thy name is no longer hallowed, Thy Kingdom is no longer so great, Thy will is no longer done either on earth or on the waters. Give us our bread which on every side we lack. Forgive our enemies who have beaten us, and not Thy generals who allowed them to do so. Do not succumb to all the temptations of the Maintenon..." *Paris mock prayer to Louis, 1709.*

Above A confused scene at the Battle of Malplaquet as the Dutch (left, English (centre) and Austrians (right) attack a little hill held by the French. *Opposite* Louis, with generals and members of the royal family, directing the bombardment of the city of Mons.

Marlborough's forces, losing only 10,000 themselves. The Allies claimed a hollow "victory," being left holding the battlefield, but the French were encouraged to find that Marlborough was not completely unbeatable.

Unlike Louis, the English and the Dutch were not looking for glory or conquest, but were fighting largely to protect their commerce and their colonies. Now that France had been weakened, further war began to seem purposeless.

When the Whigs lost power in London, Marlborough's day was done, and the new Tory government was willing to negotiate. In 1712 a truce was signed between France and England at Utrecht. Villars' victory at Denain in July convinced the Dutch that they should make peace, too. When Philip V of Spain gave up his claim to the French crown, the Peace of Utrecht was signed in 1713. Only the Empire fought on, but more victories by Villars brought them to agree to the Treaty of Rastadt in 1714.

In these treaties, France kept her frontiers intact, retaining Alsace and Strasbourg, but giving up large parts of Canada to England. Louis also recognized George of Hanover as heir to the throne of England, and gave up his support for the Stuart pretenders. Spain lost the Netherlands, Milan, Naples and Sardinia to the Empire, but this loss of land she could not control was a benefit. There was also a commercial clause in the treaty, which Louis hoped would help French trade to recover from high taxation and the loss of the Huguenots. Unfortunately for France it was rejected by the English Parliament, partly because it was opposed by the community of Huguenot exiles in London.

To both sides the Treaties brought satisfaction. France had avoided the complete humiliation threatened in 1709, and kept her claimant on the Spanish throne. The Grand Alliance was content in having set limits to the hungry demands of the Sun King.

15 The Sinking Sun

LOUIS, SEEMING IMMORTAL TO HIS COURT, lived on into an old age shadowed not only by defeat and the suffering of his people, but also by personal sorrows within his own family. He changed considerably in the last decade of his reign. The mighty Sun King suffered from depression: "Sometimes he has a fit of crying that he cannot control, sometimes he is not well," wrote Madame de Maintenon; "He has no conversation." Convinced that God was punishing him for past misdeeds, he became more humble. He cut down the luxury of his court and himself seemed "one of the soberest men in the kingdom." He abandoned his schemes for new palaces, and found fresh pleasure in his gardens. Where he had once appeared in magnificent costume, he now wore a simple brown suit and a short wig.

The court routine remained as rigid as ever. Louis still attended council in the morning and hunted each afternoon. His health was good, despite the dreadful medical treatment of the time which advised bleeding and purging for every complaint. Although he had long since lost all his teeth, he still ate heartily. Flattery within his court reached new heights in his last years. Caught in the rain in his Palace garden, a bishop declared, "The rain at Marly is never wet." Louis became a God-like being, as letters of the time reveal: "I would as soon die as spend two or three months without seeing the King," wrote the Duc de Richelieu, while Marshal de Villeroi, a general restored to favour in 1712, commented: "I begin to see Heaven open before me. The King has granted me an audience." Another general referred to Louis as his "adorable

Above A Dutch cartoon shows Louis in retreat in his old age.

"**The great men make a huge circle at the foot of the altar and you can see them standing there, their backs turned deliberately from the priest and the holy mysteries, and their faces lifted towards the King, seen kneeling on a dais, and it would seem that on him are fixed all their hearts and souls.**" *De la Cour, a courtier, describing "King-worship" in Versailles chapel.*

85

Above Peter the Great, the Tsar who had made Russia a more powerful country and tried to "westernize" Russian society, meets the future Louis XV on a visit to Paris.

master," who "knows better than we do ourselves what our needs are." Louis was simply "like God."

Louis' own complacency was shattered by the tragic sequence of sudden deaths in his family. In 1695, when his grandson had come of age, Louis had been triumphant: never before in French history had there been a King, King's son and King's grandson alive and fit to govern. With this line of Bourbons stretching ahead, there seemed no fear of an insecure future. But in 1711 the King's eldest son, the Dauphin, suddenly died of smallpox. Amiable, plump, always dutiful,

"Monseigneur" had spent a quiet lifetime over-shadowed by his father, whom he deeply respected. Worse followed. The new Dauphin, Louis' grandson, was young and hard-working (he predicted that he would be "Louis the Learned"). His wife, Marie Adelaide, an Italian princess, gay and intelligent, was deeply loved by the King. In 1712 both husband and wife died of scarlet fever, and were followed to the grave by their eldest son. Three future kings of France had died in a single year. The death of the young Dauphine was the hardest blow for Louis, "the only sorrow the King ever felt." In the bitterness of the tragedy, accusations of poisoning flew round the court: the King's nephew, Philippe, Duc d'Orleans, was par-ticularly suspected. Louis's single direct heir was now his great-grandson, the two-year-old Duc d'Anjou.

In the summer of 1715 it was noticed that Louis's appetite was fading, that he fell asleep at entertain-ments, that he suddenly looked his age. In foreign capitals bets were placed that he would not last the year. By August he was forced to take to his bed. To the

> "There are few examples of such disasters as have befallen me as the loss in one week of a grandson, a grand-daughter-in-law, and their son, all of great promise and most dearly loved. God is punishing me. I deserve it. I shall suffer the less in the next world." *Louis to Marshal Villars 1712.*

> "The whole court was enlivened by her youth and high spirits. She flitted hither and thither like a nymph, like a summer breeze . . . When they were in private, she chattered, skipped and frolicked round them (the King and his wife) sometimes perching on the arm of their chairs, sometimes on their knees. She used to fling her arms round their necks, kissing and hugging them, rumpling them . . . With her death, all joy vanished from the court, all pleasures, entertainments and delights were overcast . . . She was its light and its life . . ." *Saint-Simon on the Duchesse of Bourgogne, the Dauphine who died in 1712.*

Left Louis on his deathbed, surrounded by bishops, monks and priests.

> "My child, you are about to become a great King. I have been too fond of building; try not to fall into the same mistake. And I have been too fond of war; try to live at peace with your neighbours. Render unto God that which is God's: remember what he has done for you, and see that your subjects do Him honour. Try to take some of the burden off your people, which, unhappily, I have failed to do . . ." *Louis XIV's last words to his heir.*

last, he proudly insisted on dining in public, though, noted Saint-Simon, "I saw that he could only swallow liquids, and that it distressed him to be looked at." His will, appointing a Council of Regency during Louis XV's minority, had already been made. On 24th August the black spots of gangrene were noticed on his leg. Despite growing pain, he spent his last days giving final advice to the boy Dauphin and talking to his wife: "I thought it would be harder to die than this; I assure you that it is not a very terrible business; it does not seem difficult to me at all." On 30th August, he spoke his last words: "O My God, come to my help, haste thee to help me." Louis XIV died on 1st September 1715, aged seventy-seven, after a reign of seventy-two years, the longest in European history.

Despite his achievements in building a powerful new France, able to compete with and sometimes to dominate other great European states, the defects of his own methods – his obsession with war, with personal grandeur, with religious unity – virtually destroyed, by 1715, what he and his Ministers had built. His system, made around his proud, dominant personality and symbolized in his great Palaces, did not long survive him. The veneration of the monarchy by the people, already weakened by the hardships of the War of Spanish Succession, turned to hatred under his descendants. Under the Regency during Louis XV's minority, the Parlements regained their political power. The nobles, too, reasserted themselves against the royal Intendants. Louis himself, who reigned until 1774, proved to be a shy, ineffectual figure. Further wars – with England over colonies, and with the rising power of Prussia – sapped the French economy and pushed taxation to still more oppressive levels. At court Madame de Pompadour, the King's beautiful mistress, dominated a corrupt society. The prestige and power of the monarchy decayed further under Louis XVI (1754–93), who neglected his royal duties in his passions for hunting and locksmithery. His wife Marie Antoinette made herself unpopular by her wild spending and devotion to a life of pleasure. Blind to necessary reforms and the hardships suffered by his subjects, Louis went on trying to rule as an absolute monarch. The machinery of government fell out of gear. Financial collapse, brought on by the American War of Independence, and republican ideas from the same source, hastened the end. Revolution came in 1789, and in 1793 the guillotine sliced off the head of Louis XVI and the first French republic was born.

Below The Bourbon monarchs became even less popular with the poor of France after Louis' death, and Louis shared in the general hatred. Here, his statue is torn down from its plinth by a revolutionary Paris mob in 1792.

Table of Dates

1638   (5 September) Birth of Louis, Dauphin of France.

1643   Accession of Louis XIV. Regency of Anne of Austria.

1648   The Fronde of the Parlements. Peace of Westphalia.

1652   End of the Fronde.

1659   Peace of the Pyrenees between France and Spain.

1660   Marriage of Louis XIV to Maria-Teresa of Spain.

1661   Death of Mazarin. Beginning of Louis' personal rule.

1663   Company of the East established.

1665   Death of Philip IV of Spain.

        Colbert appointed Controller General of Finance.

        War of Devolution: invasion of Flanders.

1668   Triple Alliance (Holland, England, Sweden) against France.

1672   French attack on Holland: dykes breached.

        Louvois appointed to Council.

1678   Treaty of Nijmegen.

        The *régale* quarrel with the Pope.

1680   Persecution of Huguenots: the *dragonnades*.

1681   The Réunions: Strasbourg seized.

1682   Court moves to Versailles.

1683   Death of Maria-Teresa. King's secret marriage to Mme de Maintenon.

1685   Revocation of the Edict of Nantes.

1686   League of Augsburg against France.

1688	"Glorious Revolution" – William of Orange becomes King of England.
1689	Sack of the Palatinate.
1697	Peace of Ryswick.
1700	Death of Charles, King of Spain. Louis' grandson accepts crown.
1701	The Grand Alliance against France.
1702	War of the Spanish Succession.
1704	Battle of Blenheim.
1706	Battle of Ramillies.
1708	Battle of Oudenarde.
1709	"The Great Winter" – famine in France. Battle of Malplaquet.
1710	Famine and unrest: new taxes in France.
1711–12	Utrecht negotiations. Death of several heirs to French crown. French victory at Denain.
1713	Treaty of Utrecht.
1714	Treaty of Rastadt.
1715	(1 September) Death of Louis XIV.

Principal Characters

The French Court

    Louis XIV 1638–1715 King of France

    Maria Teresa 1638–1683 Queen of France: daughter of Philip IV of Spain

    Madame de Maintenon 1635–1719 Second wife of Louis XIV

    Anne of Austria 1601–1666 Mother of Louis XIV

    Louis, Dauphin of France 1661–1711 Son of Louis XIV

Ministers and Generals

    Cardinal Richelieu 1585–1642 Minister of Louis XIII

    Cardinal Mazarin 1602–1661 Minister to Louis XIV in his minority

    Colbert, Jean 1619–1693 Minister of Finance

    le Tellier, Michel 1603–1685 Secretary of State and War

    Louvois, François 1641–1691 Secretary of State and War

    Hugues de Lionne 1611–1671 Secretary of foreign affairs

    Turenne 1611–1675 Marshal of France

    Vauban, Sebastien, Henri, Vicomte de 1633–1707 Military Engineer

    Villars, Charles, Duc de 1653–1734 Marshal of France

Foreign Allies and Enemies

    Charles II 1630–1685 King of England

    Charles II 1661–1670 Last Hapsburg of Spain

William of Orange 1650–1702 Dutch Leader, then King of England

John Churchill, Duke of Marlborough 1650–1722 English General

James II King of England 1633–1701 exiled to France

Below Louis with the ladies of the court, from the annual Almanac for 1667.

Further Reading

There are few books about Louis XIV suitable for younger readers. The following might be used for reference:

The Seventeenth Century in France, J. Boulenger (Capricorn Books 1963). An attractive, pleasantly written general history.

The Splendid Century, W. H. Lewis (Eyre and Spottiswoode 1953). Interesting essays about various aspects of life in France during Louis's reign.

The Sun King, N. Mitford (Hamish Hamilton 1966). Splendid illustration in colour.

Saint-Simon at Versailles, ed. L. Norton (Hamish Hamilton 1958). The finest description of Louis by one of his courtiers (the sections on "The Character of Louis XIV" and "Louis XIV and his court" are outstanding).

Characters, Jean de la Bruyère (Penguin 1970). The sections "Of the court" and "Of Great Nobles" might be referred to.

An Introduction to Seventeenth Century France, John Lough (Longmans Green 1954). A good beginning for a more serious study of the period, with a fascinating section on court patronage of the arts.

An Adventure, Anne Moberly (Faber 1934). An extraordinary account of the haunting of Versailles. Two distinguished women describe Versailles gardens as seen in a "time-slip." A fascinating introduction to the study of the palace.

Other books for reference: *Louis XIV*, W. H. Lewis (Andre Deutsch 1959); *Louis XIV*, Vincent Cronin (Collins 1964); both popular biographies. *Louis XIV*, John Wolf (Gollancz 1968); outstanding, very detailed biography.

Index

Picture Credits

The author and publishers wish to thank the following for permission to reproduce illustrations appearing on the pages mentioned: Bulloz et Cie, *jacket front*; Mansell Collection, *jacket back, frontispiece*, 10, 15, 16, 17 *below*, 18, 19, 20, 21, 22, 25, 28 *below*, 29, 32, 34, 47, 48, 52 *below*, 53 *below*, 54, 56 *above* and *below*, 61, 62, 66, 68, 72, 73, 80, 83, 85, 87, 93; Reunion des Musees Nationaux de France, 6, 11, 12 *above*, 28 *above*, 35, 38–9, 45, 52 *above*, 53 *above*, 58, 60, 64, 67; Mary Evans Picture Library, 8, 17 *above*, 40, 69, 74, 75, 79; The British Library, 12 *below*; National Gallery, 13; Radio Times Hulton Picture Library, 14, 23, 24, 30, 31, 70, 82. The pictures on pages 9, 41, 57, 78, 86 and 89 are from the Wayland Picture Library. The maps on pages 42 and 86 were drawn by Liz Mackintosh.